Mary Rebecca Stewart Bird

Persian women and their Creed

Mary Rebecca Stewart Bird

Persian women and their Creed

ISBN/EAN: 9783743316263

Manufactured in Europe, USA, Canada, Australia, Japa

Cover: Foto ©ninafisch / pixelio.de

Manufactured and distributed by brebook publishing software (www.brebook.com)

Mary Rebecca Stewart Bird

Persian women and their Creed

Persian Women

and

Their Creed

BY

MARY R. S. BIRD
C.M.S. Missionary in Persia

LONDON
CHURCH MISSIONARY SOCIETY
SALISBURY SQUARE, E.C.
1899

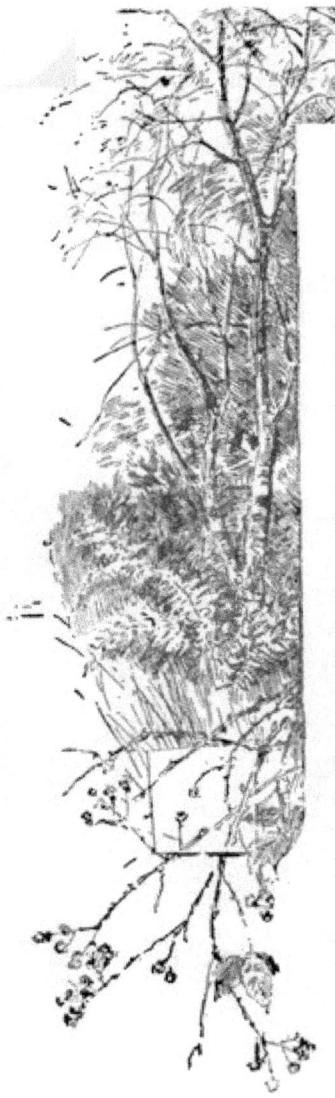

APOLOGY.

To any who may read these few pages an apology is due for having, after such a short term of service, only six years, ventured to write at all on a subject of such vast importance as work among Moslem women; a subject which involves so many difficult problems which it is quite impossible for me to solve.

Some months ago the call came through a dear wise Christian worker; but I did not want to write, and refused hastily, without consideration or prayer for God's guidance. Three times while on deputation work the request was repeated by others, who said they could not know of the spiritual needs of Persian women, having no book on this subject. Still I resisted; but at the prayer-meeting at the Leopold Rooms, before the C.M.S. Anniversary, I felt I could not really unite in the prayer for more consecration to God's will and service. He then showed me my self-will, and gave me grace to give it up and determine, should He make the way clear, to use my pen to tell of what *He* has done and is doing in a dark Moslem land.

vi   *Apology*.

May God accept this unworthy sacrifice, cleansing the offerer with the precious blood of Jesus Christ, which is all-sufficient for all sin, and of His goodness condescend to use even these weak words to rouse those who have found peace and joy through Christ to *pray* and *work* more for the poor Moslems, whom He died to save, that He may "see of the travail of His soul and be satisfied."

MARY BIRD.

Edinburgh, August, 1898.

CONTENTS.

CHAPTER	PAGE
I.—Darkness and Light .	1
II.—Darkness Rather than Light	5
III.—Daybreak in One Moslem Land .	16
IV.—Wayside Impressions .	22
V.—Work at Julfa .	34
VI.—Isfahan .	53
VII.—Scattered Seeds .	69
VIII.—Stone Made Ready	80

LIST OF ILLUSTRATIONS.

	PAGE
A Persian Fruit Shop	*Frontispiece*
A Persian	1
View of Soh	3
A Mohammedan	5
Minarets of a Mosque from which the Call to Prayer is chanted	6
"Kajāvās"	8
Persian Village Woman in House Dress	10
A Persian Family	13
The Rev. Canon Robert Bruce, D.D.	16
The late Bishop French	21
A "Takht-i-Ravân"	22
A Pass in the Mountains	24
A "Caravanserai"	26
A Caravan in the Desert	27
Mosque at Kûm	30
Group of Persian Women of a Wandering Tribe	32
A Rocky Peak near Julfa	34
A Group of Armenians	36
A View of Julfa	38
A Group of Patients at the Hospital	41
Persian Woman in Out-door Dress	45
Patients arriving at Julfa Hospital	48
A Persian Woman	53
Brass Workers, Isfahan	54
Beating out Cotton Wool	56
Interior of well-to-do Persian House	59
Smoking the Kaliān	64
Bakers' and Grocers' Shops	66
View near Isfahan	68
A Persian Village	70
Interior of Village House—Women Spinning and Knitting	72
A Persian Family	73
In the Harvest-field	76
Unequally Yoked	77
Bread-making and Baking	78
Wall surrounding a Village	84
A Beggar in a Street in Persia	89
Cooking in the Street in a Persian City	93
One of Hamedeh's Letters	96
A Mohammedan School	103

Persian Women and their Creed

CHAPTER I.

DARKNESS AND LIGHT.

A PERSIAN.

IT is written that "the evening and the morning were the first day." This divine order knows no change; we trace it throughout the whole Bible, an ever-increasing light shining through the patriarchs, psalmists, and prophets until the "Light of the World," the "Light of Men," the "True Light," the "Light of Life" came, in order that, as He Himself said, "Whosoever believeth on Me should not abide in darkness." Even then those who followed on to know the Lord were promised a fuller revelation through the teaching of His Holy Spirit (John xiv. 26), when, the veil of sin, unbelief, and superstition being removed, they with "open face beholding as in a glass the glory of the Lord," should be "changed into the same image from glory to glory, even as by the Spirit of the Lord," and were enabled to look beyond this present life, where, after all, "we see through a glass darkly," to the "then face to face," in that city where there is "no need of the sun, neither of the moon . . . the glory of God did lighten it, and the Lamb is the light thereof"—"there shall be no night there."

The glimpse of this glorious unshadowed light of heaven dazzles us, and we turn to look around on this earth where God commanded, "Let there be light," to find it is almost eclipsed. It is true His sun still rises "on the evil and on the good," a silent witness to God's faithfulness and mercy. The Sun of Righteousness has risen "to give light to them that sit in darkness and in the shadow of death"; but a veil of sin—gross sin (as well as the refined forms, which are *just as sinful and black in God's sight*, of pride of intellect, agnosticism, and self-love)—has come between man and the True Light, and again we see men "loving *darkness* rather than light, because their deeds are evil." In how many countries is this the case. Palestine, Syria, Asia Minor, parts of Persia, Arabia, and North Africa once had Gospel light; now they are given over almost entirely to the rule of the false prophet Mohammed.

But you may ask, how was it that nations which had the light should have turned again to darkness? Alas! the Christians had forgotten our Lord's solemn warning (John xii. 35) : "Walk while ye have the light, lest darkness come upon you." Instead of being "one" (John xvii. 21) in that holy bond of love which is as the cement uniting all the living stones of Christ's temple, they were torn asunder by unhappy divisions; false doctrine regarding the Trinity, the divinity of our Lord and His incarnation, had been accepted by some; others had allowed themselves to be so engrossed with ceremonies, gorgeous ritual, adoration of images and pictures, &c., that the spirit and life of Christianity was gone, and the way prepared for any false prophet.

VIEW OF SOH, A TOWN OF PERSIA.

It is on this very account that all Christians ought specially to pray and use every means in their power to take away the stumbling-block put by early Christians in the way of those who were, like the Zoroastrians, seeking after "light, more light." We have indeed need to pray in the words of the Communion Service, "Have mercy upon us, most Merciful Father; for Thy Son our Lord Jesus Christ's sake, forgive us all that is past." Our spiritual forefathers were "verily guilty"; *are we less so?* Freely *we have* received, have *we freely* given the Gospel light to the 175,000,000 of Moslems?

A Moslem woman in the Julfa Women's Dispensary asked me just after the morning prayers, "Do you believe that Book is true?" "Yes, I do, for it is God's Book, and He cannot lie," I replied. In a bitter tone she exclaimed, "Then if you believe it is true, why did you not come to tell us sooner?" Why?

Christendom was in this sad dark state when Mohammed declared himself to be the "Apostle of God," the "seal of the prophets"; and, claiming that God had revealed and was still revealing the truth to him, invited men to join the faith of Islam,* i.e. that of those who had surrendered their will to God.

Mohammed was then forty years old, and had had opportunities of studying not only the idolatrous worship of the Koreish (to which tribe he belonged), but of the Jews and Syrian Christians with whom he had come in contact when on trading expeditions with his uncle. At the beginning of his mission he tried to conciliate all of them by introducing some of their creeds and customs into the new faith; for instance, the practice of going round the Ka'abah, performed by Mecca pilgrims, was an old Koreish rite. For some time Jerusalem was declared to be the "Qiblah," the place to which all should turn when at prayer; but when Mohammed found the Jews and Christians were not joining him in any numbers he changed it to Mecca.

* Arabic verb سلم to surrender.

A MOHAMMEDAN.

CHAPTER II.

DARKNESS RATHER THAN LIGHT.

YOU know Mohammedans have as the symbol of their faith the crescent moon. A truer one could not have been found, for, like the crescent, the Moslem religion has but a little light, and much shadow, and its light, like that of its symbol, is a reflected one borrowed from the Jewish and Christian religions. In order to see this the better, shall we look at the five points of the Moslem faith, which every true believer must accept?

I. The "Kalimeh," the word, or creed, "I declare that there is no God but God; I declare that Mohammed is the apostle of God." Truth and falsehood declared in one breath!

The Moslem's Call to Prayer.

II. Prayer. Moslems are bound to repeat their prayers five times a day: at daybreak, noon, before sunset, during the short twilight, and an hour after night has begun. The first sound at daybreak in a Moslem land is the solemn call to prayer chanted by the Moazzem from the minaret or roof of the mosque. The translation of it is, " God is most great " (repeated four times), " I declare that there is no God but God ; I declare that Mohammed is the Apostle of God " (repeated twice), " Come to prayer " (twice), " Come to the refuge " (twice), " God is most great " (twice) ; adding at the daybreak call, " Prayer is better than sleep," followed by the final declaration of God's greatness.

MINARETS OF A MOSQUE FROM WHICH THE CALL TO PRAYER IS CHANTED.

Vain Repetitions.

Wherever Mohammedans may be, the moment they hear the call to prayer they lay aside any work in which they are engaged, and, after performing the ceremonial ablutions as enjoined by Mohammed (using sand if unable to procure water in the desert), turn the face to Mecca and begin to repeat their prayers, bowing, prostrating, touching the ground with the forehead, and rising again at the proper moment, with the utmost gravity and devoutness. Yet they are but "vain repetitions"; the greater proportion of the Moslems (at least, in Persia) not understanding Arabic, the "language of God and paradise," in which all their prayers are repeated. They are taught that a mistake in form or position renders the prayer valueless, e.g. "Resting on the arms when at prayer is pleasing to the people of hell." The place, too, where it is offered affects its value; one prayer said in the holy mosque at Mecca is worth 1000 repeated in any other part of the world; one in an ordinary mosque equals twenty-five said in a private house or in the bazaar.

To a Mohammedan prayer is all *duty;* not the happy communing of a child with its Father, nor the child's cry of sorrow or need to the One Who it knows is always able and willing to help. The result is that no power to change the life is gained, no fresh lesson as to how to gain the victory over besetting sin learnt. The Moslem, having completed his duty, returns to the doubtful, sinful pleasure, to lying, hard bargaining, self-indulgence, injustice, and cruelty.

III. The payment of legal, and also of voluntary, alms of camels, oxen, sheep, money, corn, dates, raisins, and of any wares sold. This duty is much insisted on in the Qur'ân; the Khalif Omar said, "Prayer carries us half-way to God; fasting brings us to the door of His palace; and alms procures admission." What a contrast from St. Peter's teaching in Acts viii. 21, where the *heart* being right in

Travelling to Mecca.

"KAJĀVĀS."

God's sight is clearly shown to be what is pleasing to Him.

IV. The Pilgrimage to Mecca, which every true believer in Islam ought to undertake. It is an imposing sight to see a party of pilgrims starting from a large town such as Isfahan. The *mullās* (Moslem priests) ride ahead of the procession with banners and trumpets, followed by the wealthy pilgrims, the men riding, the women usually in "Kajāvās," a mode of conveyance which has the appearance of two dog-kennels, one of which is strapped on either side of a mule's pack-saddle; the poor on foot, gladly spending the savings of many years and enduring great hardships to earn heaven and have a right to the title of "Hāj," which no one who has not visited Mecca may adopt. Should any of them die during the journey, the friends comfort each other with the blessedness of those who perish while on the sure and holy road to heaven.

Arrived at Mecca, the first day is spent in seven times compassing the "Ka'abah," the holy mosque, kissing the famous "black stone," and drinking water from the "Zem Zem well," which is in the Ka'abah enclosure, and is declared to be the very spring of water which sprang up when Ishmael was dying of thirst. The water is considered very holy; a small quantity is often bottled and brought back by pilgrims, either to keep for themselves or to give to friends who have been unable to visit the well. The custom of running between the mountains of Safâ and Merwâ is said to date from the time of Hagar, and to be kept up in her memory; the pilgrims walk slowly across the plain till they come to a place where there are two pillars, then they run, stopping from time to time to look around as Hagar doubtless did when seeking water for Ishmael. Mina and Arafât are also visited, and the night spent at the latter place in prayer and reading the Qur'ăn. At daybreak the following morning the pilgrims go to the sacred monument, and then hasten to the Mina Valley to hurl seven stones at three pillars to drive away the devil, as they say Abraham did when the devil tempted him not to offer up his son. Next the great sacrifices are offered (only told me by women, I have not been able to prove the statement yet), when at least 30,000 worshippers must be present or the sacrifice cannot take place. Moslems add that, should the number fall short, God in His mercy will send angels disguised as men to supplement the pilgrims, and enable them to proceed with their sacrifice.

When it is over, the men who during this sacred time have not shaved their heads nor cut their nails, to show that they have been oblivious to all earthly concerns, now do so, burying the hair and nails in the valley before returning to the world. The farewell visit to the Ka'abah is paid, and the great pilgrimage is over. Its effect, according to the Arabic proverb, is, "If your friend has been to Mecca, trust him not. If he has been there twice, avoid him. But if he made the pilgrimage the third time, flee from him, as you would from Satan."

V. Fasting during the month Ramadhan from daybreak to sunset, or as the Qur'ân expresses it, "Eat and drink until ye can plainly distinguish a white thread from a black by the daybreak, then keep the fast until night." Not only no solid food, but what is a much greater privation in a hot country, no liquid must be taken and no pipe smoked. Only sick people and

PERSIAN VILLAGE WOMAN IN HOUSE-DRESS.

travellers are exempted from this rule, and "They shall fast an equal number of other days" during the year.

This religion of works, which are not the outcome of faith, but rather the attempt on man's part to propitiate an offended deity, has little practical effect on the life, and brings *no happiness* to its followers, as they often acknowledge. For instance, a *mirza* (teacher), when reading, merely as a lesson with one of the lady missionaries, the Gospel of St. John, exclaimed, " Your religion is all happiness; ours is all weeping." A village woman visiting me asked in surprise how I could be happy when far away from all my relatives and friends. On my telling her she had made a mistake, my best Friend was always with me, she got up, and after looking behind the curtains and in my cupboard and finding no one, sat down, remarking, "I have found you out, that is a lie, there is no one here." After hearing of the Unseen " Friend, who sticketh closer than a brother," who has promised "I will not leave you orphans" (the Persian rendering is the same as the R.V.), she exclaimed, " What! your *religion* gives you happiness? Ours gives us none." Do you ask why it does not? Read the Qur'ân (their sacred book) and you will find the Moslem's god is not " love," but rather a dreaded despotic ruler to be feared. They dare not approach Him with the title Father, it would be blasphemy, they are not his children. God is their Creator and Master; they His creatures and slaves.

They do not believe that Jesus is the Son of God, "very God" as well as "very man," but only accept Him as one of the great prophets. They deny His crucifixion,* His one

---

* Moslems say either the crucifixion was a phantom, or that Judas Iscariot was transformed, becoming so like his Lord that he was mistaken for Him, and in spite of his protestations as to his identity, was crucified in Christ's place.

perfect and sufficient sacrifice for the sins of the whole world, and therefore they deny His resurrection. They do not believe in the Holy Spirit, confusing Him with Gabriel, and applying the promise of His Pentecostal coming to Mohammed himself.

They deny the genuineness of the Bible, saying that the Christians have altered it, though *when*, they are unable to declare. If they say before Mohammed's time, then why did he say it was from God? If, after the seventh century, the earlier manuscripts are sufficient proof that their statement is false. Again, they say each revelation abrogated the former one, that Moses' law was superseded by Christ's Gospel, and the Gospel by the Qur'ân, which was revealed to Mohammed, "the seal of the prophets"; that each of these revelations was in its own time the true guide to salvation, the Qur'ân being now the only and final one.

One proof Moslems give of the Qur'ân being a revelation direct from God is the beauty of its language, surpassing any human composition, and this is always declared to be a miracle. Yet it is historically inaccurate; for instance, the Virgin Mary is said to be the sister of Aaron; and Haman the contemporary of Moses! It is also full of contradictions.

Paradise to which all Moslems are to be admitted in the after-life is not a place where perfect communion with God, unmarred by sin, will give pleasure for evermore; but rather a land of sensual delights without restriction, where wine (forbidden by Mohammed) may be drunk, and the utmost license indulged in. The "meanest of the people will see his gardens, wives, servants, and other possessions occupy the space of 1000 years' journey"; seventy tables, each with seventy dishes of food, will be served at one time; "if he desires fruit, the boughs of the trees will bend down so that he may the more readily gather it; if a bird, it shall

The Fruit of Religion.   13

fall ready roasted at his feet." So that he may be able to enjoy all, "the ability of one hundred men in eating and drinking will be granted to one."

In St. Matthew vii. 15—20 our Lord tells us plainly how the false is to be distinguished from the true: "the good tree bringeth forth good fruit." Which religion brings forth good fruit, Christianity or Mohammedanism? Listen to the testimony of two Moslems, one a man, the other a woman. The former said, "Show me what your faith does. You say you do not believe in works of supererogation nor in pilgrimages; your faith does nothing." After hearing of the "expulsive power of the new affection," and the fruit of the Spirit, he exclaimed, "Love, mercy, truth, purity, we *talk* of these, but have *not* got them." The woman asked for St. Matthew vii. to be read to her; verses 19 and 20 struck

A PERSIAN FAMILY.

her greatly, and she too said our religion had no fruit. Being told it had, she again repeated her statement; running quickly over the five points of the Moslem faith, she proved that Christians observed none (a Christian's prayers being unavailing because not offered aright, and alms valueless on account of not being paid to *mullās*). "Yes," she said, "I repeat it, I said the truth; your religion has *no fruit*." Asking her not to trust to human testimony, but listen to the inspired Word of the God of truth, I read Gal. v. 22—26. The Word which is still "quick and powerful," touched her, and she said, "Do you want to know what the Moslem faith teaches its followers to do? To oppress the widow, to devour the orphan's property, to be most unjust to a stranger or any one who is without protection, to think nothing of poisoning a friend or one who has served them faithfully, if by so doing they can annex some property or in any way enrich themselves." Alas! this statement is only too true.

Shall we pause a moment to consider the oft-repeated statement that "the Moslem faith is a very good one," sometimes qualified by "for those people"? Mohammed undoubtedly began life with good intentions, but puffed up by pride (as he must have been, or how could he have dared to mention his own apostleship at the same time as the unity of God?), instead of, in humble dependence upon God, seeking to reform his own and other tribes, he sought personal power. At the first he made, as we have already seen, great efforts to gain the help of the Jews and Christians; later, the Arabs, being naturally warlike, were attracted to his standard by the hope of fame and plunder in the holy wars. Emboldened by success, Mohammed taught his people to show no mercy; the sword and faith of Islam *were* and *are* inseparable; at the point of the sword the alternative was offered either to repeat the "Kalimeh" or die as an unbeliever. Take, for example, the case of Abu Sofian, who, when asked by Mohammed,

"Dost thou believe that I am the apostle of God?" replied, "Thou art more dear to me than father or mother, but I swear by God I am at present in doubt of thy apostleship." Hearing this, Abbas said, "Woe be to thee; become a Moslem and say, 'I declare that there is no God but God; I declare that Mohammed is the apostle of God,' or your head shall be cut off." On hearing this Abu Sofian at once believed!

Unbelievers when invited to become Moslems were promised protection should they do so, but should they refuse they were to be put to death and their families to be made slaves. Nations were dealt with by Mohammed's followers in the same manner. For instance, in the time of Yezdigird, Saad-ibn-Abu Wakass, the Arab general, sent ambassadors bidding the Persians accept the faith of Islam; on their refusing, war was declared, the battle of Kadisia was fought, when the Persian royal standard was taken. At the second invasion, in the twenty-first year of the Hijrah, Persia was conquered; the people, who were Zoroastrians, fled to India and Beluchistan, or from fear became Moslems. Are such deeds a recommendation to any religion? And yet they have been repeated in Syria, Egypt, the Soudan, Arabia, &c. Contrast the spread of Christianity: no force but that of the "Sword of the Spirit" has been used, but wherever Christian soldiers have faithfully wielded that weapon, sounding the Gospel trumpet call, "Come," for "God so *loved* the world that He gave His only begotten Son, that whosoever believeth on Him should *not perish*, but have everlasting life," victory has been granted them. *Life*, not death, marks the way of the Captain of our Salvation; liberty to the captives, not slavery and oppression. Surely no Christian will ever again declare a faith which bears such fruit as that of the Moslem, and which yet denies the need of atonement, "good enough" for one single immortal soul for whom Christ died and whom He is yearning to save.

THE REV. CANON
R. BRUCE, D.D.

CHAPTER III.

DAYBREAK IN ONE MOSLEM LAND.

WILL you travel in thought to a Moslem land that we may together see the streaks of dawn there? In 1811 Henry Martyn heard God calling him from India to Persia, and obeyed. The greater part of the year was spent at Shiraz, where he worked hard amid great difficulties and much opposition, daily meeting the *mullās* and all who cared to visit him, endeavouring to point them to the truth. His courage and faithfulness struck them greatly, as well as his piety, and were long remembered by them. But his greatest work was the translation of that Word, " the entrance of which giveth light." Henry Martyn completed the New Testament and the Psalms,* and set out the following year to present the precious volume to the Shah, who was then at Tabriz,

---

* Dr. W. Glen, of the Scottish Missionary Society at Kerak, Astrakhan, took up and completed the work Henry Martyn had begun. In 1846, at Edinburgh, Henry Martyn's translation of the Psalms and New Testament, with the remainder of the Old Testament translated by Dr. Glen, was printed. A copy of this first complete Persian Bible was presented to the late Shah, Nasar-ud-deen, on his accession to the throne in 1848.

intending to proceed from there to England. Suffering terribly from fever, ague, and consumption, he struggled on until he arrived at Tokat, in Armenia, where, with only his two Armenian servants, with no true Christian friend to minister to him, surrounded by the Moslems for whom he was sacrificing his life, he finished his fight and won the victor's crown at the early age of thirty-one. The closing sentence of his last letter, written only ten days before his death, was, "When shall time give place to eternity? When shall appear that new heaven and new earth wherein dwelleth righteousness? Then there shall in no wise enter in anything that defileth; none of that wickedness which has made men worse than wild beasts, none of those corruptions which add still more to the miseries of mortality shall be seen or heard of any more." Shall we call his a lost life? No, indeed, for to quote his own words, "The Word of God has found its way into Persia, and it is not in Satan's power to oppose its progress if the Lord hath sent it."

This first "white line" which we can distinguish amid the blackness of Mohammedanism remains—"He being dead yet speaketh." After a long time the light began very slowly to increase.

In 1833 the American Presbyterians established a Mission among the Nestorian and Turkish-speaking peoples of Urumiah, but there was no Mission of any Christian body to the Persians until Dr. Bruce, who had previously been at work for ten years among Mohammedans in the Punjab and on the Afghan frontier, went to Persia in 1869 to perfect himself in Persian, which would be of great use among the Afghans, and to distribute Henry Martyn's translation of the New Testament among the Persians. When Dr. Bruce consulted the Rev. Henry Venn about returning to Derajat *viii* Persia, that veteran soldier of the Cross surprised him. Mr. Venn's eyes filled with tears, and he said, "Oh, do go to Persia; I am so thankful for this opening: it is one of those things we looked for in vain in times past, but God is giving us now."

The subsequent history of the Persia Mission has proved that where the first of the "Missionary Principles" laid down by the Rev. John Venn on March 18th, 1799, "Follow God's leading," is carried out, God does direct His servants. Dr. and Mrs. Bruce were indeed led by God to select Julfa, the Armenian suburb of Isfahan, as the place to begin work for Him.

For two years there seemed to be no hope of the Society taking up permanent work in Persia. Dr. and Mrs. Bruce had just determined to proceed to the Derajat, when, to their amazement, a letter from Mr. Venn reached them in March, 1871, saying, "If you can see your way to make a good revision of Henry Martyn's version of the New Testament, stay in Persia; if not, go on to India." At that time it took five or six months to get a reply from England, so the missionaries were cast upon God alone for counsel. They earnestly prayed for guidance, and in the month of April nine Moslems asked for baptism. This prolonged their stay till instructions could be received from the London Committee.

During the summer of 1871 it became evident that the famine which had caused such suffering during the previous winter would become much more severe; not that the harvest was such a failure, but the crops were seized and stored by the wealthy, and only sold to the perishing people at famine prices. No appeal was made for funds, but earnest prayers were offered to Him whose are the silver and the gold, in answer to which over 16,000*l.* were received from India,

Germany, and England, by means of which thousands of lives were saved. The most extraordinary incident was the collecting of 6300*l*. in Wurtemburg by Pastor Haas, of Ludwigsburg, who, after having sent the first instalment of 1000*l*., wrote, saying, "We know that Mohammed taught his followers to hate Christians, but Jesus taught us to love our enemies. We have collected this money in sixpences and shillings (as it were) from the poor Germans, and we wish it to be distributed without distinction of creed or race to Christians, Jews, and Moslems." Would that you could have sat with me in many a humble mud house in Isfahan and its neighbourhood, and heard the people acknowledge how Dr. Bruce had saved their lives, or Mrs. Bruce clothed them and dressed their wounds. Even a hard Moslem heart can be touched, and such deeds are not soon forgotten. After twenty-seven years the name of "Kishish Sâhib" (clergyman Sâhib) will awaken touching memories. One told me his father and five children had died of starvation before Dr. Bruce heard of the case. Though it was after sunset when the news was brought to him, he at once came, bringing food with him. The mother died, but his life was saved.

But Dr. and Mrs. Bruce did not go to Persia to distribute only "the bread that perisheth," but, by God's help, to give living bread to starving souls. They fully realized that though mercy and philanthropy are fruits of the Christian religion (where the God of love is not known, there is no love for fellow-man), they are not "the power of God unto salvation." "Persia for Christ," was the motto hung over the fireplace in the doctor's study, and this was their aim and desire.

When the famine was over, Dr. Bruce proceeded with the revision, or rather retranslation, of the Persian Bible; and to this task many hours every day were devoted, God permitting him to finish, what we may rightly call, his chief and most important work.

Persia was added to the list of C.M.S. Missions in 1875. In 1880 a Medical Mission was begun, and carried on with great vigour for eight years, by the Rev. Dr. Höernle. Of the medical work being done there now we must see more later on.

Bishop French, of Lahore, visited the Mission in 1883; he confirmed sixty-nine Armenians who had joined the Mission Church, and ordained the pastor, the Rev. Minasakan George. The Bishop remained eighteen days in Isfahan, having a good opportunity of seeing something of both sides of the Persian character, for whilst mullās and inquirers came in small numbers to argue with him on religion or for instruction, the sheikh was endeavouring to forbid the sale of Bibles, "being naturally alarmed and aggravated by finding that the disposition grows to hear and receive the Word of God."

Before asking you to pass on to the more recent work, shall we face that frequently repeated question, "Is it worth while to spend so much time and trouble on such people, to say nothing of the expense?" The expense! The Bible teaches us that the value of a sinner's soul is so great in God's sight (remember, "there is no difference," English and Moslems are alike in this), that only the priceless blood of His own beloved Son could purchase it. Not all the gold created is sufficient to buy salvation for one soul. Ought we then to grudge the silver and gold for God's work? Remember, it is not ours, but His (1 Tim. vi. 7; Job i. 21). We are only trustees of it for the time being. Let the late Bishop French and Bishop Stuart reply as to time and trouble. They both, not in the flush of excitable youth, but with the matured judgment and experience of older life, resigned their sees to become missionaries in the Moslem lands of Arabia and Persia. Does not the act speak for itself? Few men care to step *down* the ladder; only those who believe the truth of our Lord's words, "I, if I be lifted up from the earth, will draw all men unto Me," can for His sake gladly say, "*He* must increase, I must decrease," counting it their highest honour to spend and be spent in His service for "such people."

THE LATE BISHOP FRENCH.

A "TAKHT-I-RAVÂN."

CHAPTER IV.

WAYSIDE IMPRESSIONS.

WOULD it help you to understand better the actual needs of Persia to-day if you were to accompany us on our way to and from Julfâ, where the C.M.S. station is, and so get a glimpse of the land, its people, and its life? I had almost written *home-life*, but this does not exist; there is no word for *home* in the Persian language, because it has not been required; the Moslems have none of the associations and tender memories which that word awakens in us.

Landing from the Russian steamer at Enzelli, on the south coast of the Caspian, we found we still had some hours of sailing in a small boat across the lagoon and up the creek to Pera-bazaar; the deep blue sky and water, the luxuriant growth of sedge-grass on the banks, and the terra-cotta coloured sails of many of the boats seen in the brilliant sunshine were lovely; the boatmen in their faded cotton coats, enlivened with patches of all colours and sizes, very picturesque. When the breeze was not sufficient to carry us along, they rowed well, refreshing themselves by eating many cucumbers. From the landing-stage we drove to Resht, a large town where much silk is woven, the town being surrounded by mulberry gardens, where quantities of silkworms are bred. Every morning we saw the men returning from collecting the cocoons, carrying them in large baskets suspended one at either end of a pole slung across the shoulders of the bearer.

Our first care was to engage a muleteer, and decide whether we would ride, sit in a "Kajává," or recline in a "Takht-i-raván"—a covered litter with shafts at either end, to which only two mules are attached, though you have the privilege of paying at the rate for four!—and settling the number of our baggage animals. Oh, the bargaining! How Easterns enjoy and excel in it! What an admirable device it is for "killing time" and testing one's stock of patience! Nearly all the animals have bells varying much in size and tone; their music is usually the only sound to be heard in the desert, and, though very monotonous, is useful, especially when travelling by night, the muleteer knowing by the bells if one of the mules has strayed to the right or left. The harness is often decorated with tassels of bright wools, and the head-gear embroidered with little white shells. Of course, charms are not forgotten, to prevent any one casting the Evil Eye on the poor beasts.

Near Resht the forest is beautiful, walnuts, planes, willows, acacias, and olive trees overgrown by vines. Persians say the vine never injures the tree it grows over. No wonder our Lord called Himself the "True Vine"; His embrace means new and more abundant life, beauty, and

A PASS IN THE MOUNTAINS.

fruitfulness. Vegetation became scarcer and the road much worse as we began to ascend the Elburz Mountains, much of the way being very rocky, sometimes smooth, sometimes in big boulders, among and over which the strong Persian horses and mules picked their way carefully and cleverly. When the mountains had been crossed, the road, or rather track, lay chiefly across the desert, with its endless ranges of bare mountains on either side. Even at the end of May the ground was dry and parched. How often we longed for "a shadow from the heat" as we crossed the plains, and realized David's intense longings after God, "As the hart panteth after the water brooks, so panteth my soul after Thee, O God."

The cup of cold water which, if taken literally, in England seems so easy to give, not involving much self-sacrifice, is there a valuable gift. Well do I remember meeting a caravan whose supply of water had run short; the children were crying with thirst, and eagerly held out their empty bottles, yet it was with difficulty that I could persuade our muleteer (Moslem) to give them any of our water.

The day's march varies considerably in length, according to the difficulties of the way and the distance apart of the towns or villages where there are caravanserais, which are certainly not up to nineteenth-century ideas of hotels; but then they are cheap; 10*d.* per night seemed the ordinary charge for a room, built of mud, festooned with cobwebs and soot, a hole in the roof to let out the smoke of the fire, a lattice, or sometimes no opening but the doorway to admit light and air, which is the more easily done when the door is missing! The caravanserais are built in the form of a large open square closed by heavy wooden doors; the rooms run round the quadrangle, the courtyard being reserved to tether the camels, horses, mules, and donkeys in; their heavy saddles are not taken off at night, and the ringing of their bells and a habit of getting loose with a view to practising fighting, help to make night lively! Bedding, cooking utensils, &c., must form part of every traveller's luggage, nothing of the sort being provided.

Wherever there is a river, and irrigation is attended to, the land is fertile, but nowhere else. We were much struck by our native servant, who would hardly notice a glorious sunset, and was silent when we admired grand rocks; but the moment he sighted a stream of water, which did not strike us as being anything beautiful or remarkable, he became eloquent. We had yet to learn no water meant

A "CARAVANSERAI."

"A CARAVAN IN THE DESERT."

no life—God grant that Persians may soon learn that no living water means perishing souls!

On the outward journey, not knowing the language, we could only look and be looked at; but even then we could realize how great was the need of spiritual water-carriers. During the twenty-one days' march from the Caspian to Julfâ, only in two places did we find Christian workers: at Resht, where one Protestant Armenian, sent by the American Presbyterian Mission in Teheran, was trying to be minister, colporteur, and schoolmaster in one; and at Teheran, where the American Presbyterians have their headquarters, they have witnessed, and are witnessing faithfully for Christ amid many difficulties and discouragements.

But what of the inhabitants of other towns and villages: are they to perish without hearing of God's love to them? Thank God, this year Mission stations have been started at Yezd, eight days' march, and Kirmān, twenty days from Julfâ, but beyond—nothing, until you reach Baghdād, on the south-west, and Quetta, on the Indian frontier.

On the return journey, having studied Persian, we could mix with the people and learn still more of their need of the Saviour. It would not be correct to say we found *many* longing for Him; until a sinner has been convinced of the sinfulness of sin by the Holy Spirit he is not likely to cry for deliverance; but many were willing to listen to the Gospel, and often we were struck by the evident craving for something more soul-satisfying than their own creed. The curiosity of the people, which we had not appreciated on our way to Julfâ, we found a real help to missionary work on our return, bringing the people together for a *tamāshá*, i.e. show. To reply to very much the same questions every day is rather wearisome, but far more than atoned for by the opportunity gained for a Scriptural object-lesson, or the repetition of one of our Lord's parables, which have such a wonderful charm for them. May we not expect that even amid the din of a Persian caravanserai some of the Good Shepherd's lost sheep may hear His voice and enter His fold?

At several of the villages near Julfâ we found old hospital and dispensary patients, who welcomed us warmly, inviting their friends to meet us, and asking for the Gospel stories they had heard before, to be read to them. We arrived at Shūr-āb ("salt-water"—we found the name was well given, the tea we bought only increasing our thirst!) a little before midnight, and found the people very friendly. Tracts were readily accepted; one person said, "We have a Book given us some years ago by a clergyman (Dr. Bruce); it is good." We asked to see it. At first they hesitated, afraid lest other travellers should arrive, but after listening and hearing no other caravan coming, they ventured to produce a well-worn copy of St. John's Gospel, and then begged for a "big Book." From another place the postman brought a letter after us asking for four more Gospels, and promising they should be read. An old coat had been sent to wrap them in, so that no one on the road might see them. At Karūd a boy training to be a reader at the mosque asked for my Gospel, which he read aloud very well, but when I asked him the meaning of the passage he promptly replied, "No Christian book has any meaning; the mullās and their disciples say so." What devices Satan has to keep the people from the truth which would make them free!

Kūm is always considered a bigoted place; hundreds of pilgrims from all parts of Persia go there to visit Fatimeh's shrine. The mosque built over this shrine is beautiful—at least the outside of it is—anyone so defiling as a Christian "dog" would never be admitted within its precincts. The shrine is immediately under the dome, which is covered with plates of gold, the gifts of the faithful. The minarets and front of the building are covered with rich-coloured tiles which harmonize in the way Eastern shades always do. A large garden of pomegranates, just then covered with their brilliant scarlet flowers, added much to the beauty of the place. Kūm, like Kirbela, is a sacred burying-place, the hope being that any one buried near a saint will, by the merit of that saint, obtain a better resurrection. We passed several caravans carrying bodies; very terrible they were, the badly-made coffins having been damaged on the way. If the deceased were wealthy, some of the relatives or servants were in attendance, with their shirts either torn or left unbuttoned,

MOSQUE AT KÛM.

according to the depth of their grief, and a white girdle or turban cloth round the neck for mourning. When the relatives are poor, or unable for any reason to go with the body, it is given in charge to the muleteer, a small sum being paid him in advance. When he returns bringing a document signed by the mullā at Kūm, stating that he has received his fee and performed the last rites for the dead, the remainder of the amount is paid to the muleteer.

Yet even in Kūm God gave us an opportunity of telling some of the women of His free salvation for them. A poor woman accidentally upset the tea urn over her little child, scalding her badly. Our servant, knowing we had ointment, brought the mother and child to us. When the wounds were dressed, I told them it was our custom to pray for and with our patients; they were willing not only for prayer, but to listen while I read of Christ blessing little children. Shortly after they left, quite a number of their friends came needing medical help, and evidently expecting teaching. One or two could read, and accepted portions of Scripture and tracts. They all returned at daybreak next day, the child and her mother so grateful for the trifling kindness, and all ready for a last lesson, and several wanting copies of "the book with a meaning" for their husbands and sons. Oh, what a responsibility it is to give a lesson, realizing it may be the only one those women will ever hear! We were continuing our journey to England, and in a few days they would be returning from the pilgrimage to their distant homes. Thankfully we gave Scripture portions to those who asked for them, telling the women they contained the secret of life, peace and joy.

In several of the villages between Teheran and Resht, Turkish is almost entirely spoken, so that we could only distribute some tracts, which were well received, the people saying they had never had any in their own language before. At Kharzan, a village high up on the Elburz Mountains, many sick people were brought to us. Both they and their friends were very ignorant of their own religion, and therefore willing to listen to "the Old, Old Story," so new to them. The mullā accepted a Gospel and tracts, which we saw him reading to a little group of friends. We shall never forget Jubilee Day, June 20th, 1897, which we spent there. At daybreak all the outlines of the mountains were indefinite and hazy; then as the sun rose above one of the mountains, each

GROUP OF PERSIAN WOMEN OF A WANDERING TRIBE.

peak stood out sharp and clear against the deep blue sky, while the valleys were still half in mist, the corn and wild flowers on the cultivated patches of ground added life and colour to the scene; at noon the sun was just overhead, its dazzling brightness penetrating everywhere, reminding one of the proverb, "When the sun is highest he casts the least shade." At sunset the beauty far surpassed description; a golden light rested on all, except the most distant ranges of mountains, which were purple and hazy again; each moment the colour grew more crimson and intense; all Nature seemed hushed by the glory of the great Creator's work; the sun sank behind a mountain, and darkness as a curtain quickly came between us and the glory. The call to prayer rang through the air, " God is most great "; whilst uniting with Moslems in prayer and praise to our one Creator, we asked, How long will it be before the Sun of Righteousness will rise in this beautiful yet benighted village?

To mention only one more incident of our journey: at Imām Zādeh, where we halted in a lovely wood, with maidenhair fern growing freely at the edge of the little brook, a Persian helped our servant to collect wood and light a fire to boil our kettle. He asked if we had any books, and gladly accepted a Gospel, promising to read it daily. Hiding it in the folds of his coat, he went away quickly, but soon reappeared with two friends, who also could read and wanted Testaments—" Big ones, and will you bring us more when you come back from London?" A wayside seed truly, but who may say to what height it may grow?

A ROCKY PEAK NEAR JULFA.

CHAPTER V.

WORK AT JULFA.

JULFA until this last year (1898) has been the only C.M.S. station in Persia. Much work for God is being carried on there. In the schools, where 205 Armenian boys and 222 girls are taught, precious seed has not only been sown, but has sprung up and is bearing fruit; all the present Sunday-school teachers were formerly pupils; nearly all the colporteurs of the British and Foreign Bible Society and the Mission agents in the hospital, &c., have been trained there. A small number of Moslem boys and girls attend whenever they can, but the mullās are very averse to their receiving instruction; several times they have all been dispersed and forbidden to return.

The Sunday morning service is well attended by the Armenian members of the congregation, as well as by an increasing number of Moslems. Bible-classes and the Sunday-school are held in the afternoon for Armenians, and separate classes for Mohammedans. Later an opportunity is given to the European residents to unite in their own language in the same beautiful liturgy as their friends in the homeland.

Visiting the congregation, as well as among outsiders, is carried on regularly. Meetings of the Y.M.C.A., Gleaners' Union, and Temperance Society are also held. The "Henry Martyn Memorial Press" has been established to meet the great need for Christian literature. Tracts, hymns, and books, written or translated by the missionaries, especially by the Rev. W. St. Clair Tisdall, who has charge of this branch of the work, will, we hope, be the means of sending the glad tidings to many who are beyond the sound of the Gospel. Inquirers are welcomed and taught whenever they come, whether day or night; visitors entertained—a duty often requiring much time and patience, Natives considering it etiquette to pay long visits—but kindness and courtesy go a long way towards breaking down prejudices, and forming friendships which afford some of the best opportunities of witnessing for our Master. Itinerating tours are made, enabling the missionaries to get into touch with some of the people far away from all light and teaching. The Medical Mission provides for the care of suffering bodies as well as souls. Whilst we thank God for what He is enabling those to do whom He has sent into this corner of His field, none are so painfully aware as the workers themselves of its littleness and the vast need of that land "created by Him and for Him," but now under the dominion of the great false prophet.

Do not let any reader run away with the impression which seems as common as it is incorrect, that if they went abroad work would be "so easy," numbers of Natives would be waiting, anxious to learn, ready to welcome a teacher, and there would be none of the old difficulties to contend with. We have already considered the case of those with whom one comes in contact for a brief half-hour when travelling; those lost and scattered sheep without any shepherds to call them back to the fold. But even where, as at Julfá, a Mission station has been established for twenty-eight years, and work

A GROUP OF ARMENIANS.

is regularly organized, still there are obstacles in the way; first and greatest, the fact that there is so little religious liberty. The law given by Mohammed is still in force: "Whoso apostatizes from his religion, let him die for it, and he is an infidel."

For any man or woman who has only just learned to trust in Christ to be told that he or she may, for no other reason than this, have at any time to face death for His sake, and if not willing for this, cannot be admitted as a member of His visible Church, is indeed a severe test. How some, through Christ's strength made perfect in their weakness, have triumphed, has at one and the same time made me rejoice, and feel the deepest shame that babes in the faith should have so far outstripped me, when my opportunities have been so much greater.

Before attempting to give some details of the Medical Mission work among the women and children, in which I was permitted to share, may I explain, to avoid any misunderstanding, that, alas! I am *not* a "qualified" person, never having had the opportunity of that training, the value of which only one who has been trying to work without having had it, can fully appreciate. Nor do I wish to advocate "quackery"; the "vessels of gold and of silver," the *best* people have to offer, are not too good for the service of our Master's house, though in His gracious, tender compassion He may condescend to use those "of wood and of earth."

When in 1891 Miss Stubbs (now in charge of the girls' school) and I were attached to the Mission, Dr. and Mrs. Bruce, the Rev. H. Carless,* and Mrs. Aidinyantz were the only missionaries. There had been no medical missionary

---

* Who on May 25th, 1898, was called from serving his Master at Kirman to His immediate presence.

A VIEW OF JULFA.

for some time, so that that work was in abeyance, and work among Moslem women had not been begun. After studying the language for some months, I began to seek openings among the women, but the door seemed closed. Three little girls said they would come for reading and knitting lessons, but they were soon frightened away by the mullā telling them it was bad for them to learn to read before they were married. Shortly after, several women asked to be shown how to knit gloves; only two persevered, still it was something to have admission to two houses where one nearly always found neighbours ready enough to talk, though not so fond of listening! During this waiting-time, when praying to God to unlock some door, He granted an answer in a most unexpected manner. Going up the street one day, I noticed a poor woman crying bitterly. Knowing she was the mother of some children who were very friendly with me, I asked her what was the matter. She said her little boy was very ill; she was willing for me to go in and see him, and I found he had a bad attack of malarial fever. After a little time I proposed prayer; the mother said it was no use, she had repeated her prayers over and over again without any effect. The boy whispered, "You pray." The women who were in the courtyard listened while, with stammering tongue indeed, I prayed that, should God see fit, He would soon restore the little boy to health, and give pardon and salvation to us all. The woman gratefully accepted quinine, &c., for him, and he quickly recovered. No sooner was he better, than the mother told all her neighbours I was a doctor. In vain I protested; Moslems rarely speak the truth themselves, and they evidently thought I would not do so either. Every day women and children came, and it seemed so clear that it was my duty to try, in the absence of skilled aid, to do what I could for the sufferers, that the women's dispensary was opened; if the women had come from a distance and wished to remain in the hospital, they were admitted.

From the first my greatest desire was to tell the sick ones of the Great Physician who still, though now invisible, goes about doing good to *soul* and body.

Many of the women resented prayer being offered in Persian, but this opposition came to an end when they saw the marvellous answers God granted us. One day in the late autumn a woman said at the conclusion of prayers, "If you believe God will hear and answer your prayers when offered in Persian, why do you not ask Him to send snow or rain to-day?" No autumnal rain had fallen, a matter of great importance, as should it fail a famine would surely be the consequence.

I told her we certainly would add this to the petitions just offered, asking God to have mercy, and whenever He saw fit, send us rain or snow, for we had no right to limit the Almighty to one day, and we again knelt for prayer. When her sick child had been attended to she left the dispensary, saying to the other women present, "You will see God will never hear nor answer her prayer." When she returned in three days for more medicine, she asked for permission to speak to the women who were there. After telling them what she had done on her previous visit, she said that before she could reach her house, about a mile and a half away, such a heavy snowstorm came on that her chuddar was wet through, adding that it seemed to her God heard and answered a Christian's prayer sooner than that of a Mohammedan.

This saying being reported by some of the women, the mullās heard of it, and issued the first prohibition against the work. It lasted nearly a fortnight, during which time only a few women ventured in when they saw no spies were in the street. The very next morning after the prohibition had been declared, the neighbouring mullā's nephew, who had been kicked by a donkey a few days before, his cheek being badly cut, came in to have it dressed, saying his mother was ill, so he had come alone. The dressing was nearly done, when an old woman appeared, saying, "Do you know of the prohibition? The women dare not come in. The order was sent last night from Isfahan to the mullā to be issued. Why, that is his nephew!" The boy laughed; evidently he knew all about it. Seeing him go out, six women ventured in. I was just dressing a burnt arm when a woman rushed in. "Go, go, the governor's head servant is in the street." In a moment the room was cleared. A little later a child came asking me to go to the desert to finish bandaging the poor arm.

Persians have a proverb, "A bad word is like the sound

Advertised the Work. 41

of a dome," i.e. it echoes back, which proved true. This prohibition, like subsequent ones, proved to be no advantage to our opposers, but rather for us, advertising the work, so that when the order was withdrawn the women came in much larger numbers. When visiting this same mullā's wife some weeks afterwards, she spoke quite openly of the

A GROUP OF PATIENTS AT THE HOSPITAL.

matter; her version of the story being that though her husband had received the order, he had *not* issued it, knowing it was a mistake!

On one occasion a woman kept repeating all prayer-time, "Jesus is your prophet, but we have a better." When I tried to explain the difference between a prophet and the Saviour, she listened willingly. Afterwards she told me she had been told to come and say this.

Some people in England seem to think "it is a hardship and unfair to *force* religion upon those who do not wish for it," but where is this done? As I often told any women who wanted to have medicine given them before prayers, "You know our rule is to have prayer and Bible teaching, yet you have come of your own accord; if you do not approve, you are free to leave us and go to your own Moslem doctors." Ought we not to apply the same reasoning to spiritual matters as to temporal? Which of us would applaud the surgeon who, rather than cause his patient an hour's suffering, refused to use the knife, but thought nothing of sacrificing his life? Would it be less culpable for missionaries to shrink from offering those who come to them a perfect cure, which has never been known to fail, because it might entail suffering for a time?

Thank God, a few of the women who used to hate the sound of the Gospel, only coming for treatment, have found in the hospital or dispensary better things than those they sought.

While many who came were indifferent, others were glad to listen. Against March 13th, 1892, there is in my diary the entry, "I was detained at the hospital this morning with a case just brought in, so was late in opening the dispensary. One woman said, 'It is late; say a short prayer.' Another exclaimed, 'If you will tell us the next story to the one we

heard last time, we will listen half an hour,' and they did"!
Under date of July 3rd, 1893, is the entry: "A small boy
was brought in with a bad wound on his head in a dreadful
state. The mother said he had screamed all night with the
pain of it. When it was dressed, I said to the child we
would ask God to give him sleep and cure him if He saw fit.
The little fellow repeated the simple prayer after me. While
waiting for a lotion to be prepared, he lay down on the floor
and fell asleep. The women present asked each other if it
was because the Christian had prayed." Again, August 14th,
1896:—"One woman said after prayers, 'I heard you read
that Book in a house in Isfahan quite six months ago; I
have been wanting one ever since. To-day I told my
neighbour I would fetch her medicine for her, so as to have
an opportunity of getting it.' She kissed the Gospel reverently
and wrapped it in a handkerchief; she did not wish
to give her name." I have not heard of her since.

Before mentioning work in the hospital, would you like to
hear one or two native remedies? For fever, mix quinine
and bitter almond oil into a paste, and rub it on the pulses.
If any one has been bitten by a dog, get some of the hair of
the *same* animal, singe it, and sprinkle the ashes on the
wound. For a burn, the ashes of a piece of calico dyed
with indigo, or an ointment composed of pomegranate juice,
white of egg, and gunpowder were well recommended, the
dressing to be either a piece of rag (it need not be clean) or
brown paper. Extra talismans, charms, and prayers should
be bought and worn by the patient. For instance, a Hāj's
baby had convulsions. The parents took it to the mullā,
who said the child was possessed; the only remedy was to
measure the child's height, and buy a prayer exactly the
same length, strap it down the child's back, and then read it
aloud, when the spirit would depart. The parents in that

particular case, finding the mullā would charge five tomans = 1*l*.) for the prayer, decided as the baby was a girl she was not worth so much! In April, 1897, a young woman suffering from suicidal mania was brought. Her friends had taken her to their doctors, who said it was no case for them, but for the mullās, who must exorcise the demon. The mullās, after the payment of 1*l*., wrote one verse of the Qur'ān on a tiny slip of paper, rolled it up, and ordered it "to be buried in her flesh in such a way that the demon might not see it." So the doctor made an incision in her arm two inches long, and deep enough for the paper to be inserted and the wound stitched up. But, alas! the place suppurated instead of healing, and the woman was no better; yet so strong was their faith in the remedy that they would not permit Dr. Carr (who by that time was in charge of the medical work) to remove it.

If it should be suspected that the malady has been caused by any one casting the "evil eye" on the patient, it is best to apply one of the tests, so that the offender being discovered the spell may be broken. The egg test is one I have seen used. An old witch brought some eggs; after a good many incantations she bid the patient and her friends name any she thought had a spite against her; as each was named a black spot was made with a piece of charcoal on the egg; names of men being marked on one side, those of women on the other. Then a brazier of charcoal was brought in, all the marked eggs were placed in it with the round end up; an invocation to the prophets was repeated while all sat round, breathlessly waiting to see which egg would crack first, and through whose spot the crack had run, that being the one who had cast the "evil eye." To break the spell the egg was thrown in running water. If that should be too far away it may be cast out in the street.

Happy Hours.

Many happy hours were spent morning and evening at the hospital, doing what I could for the souls and bodies of the poor sufferers. Often when they first arrive they are so bigoted as to refuse to eat food prepared in the hospital, or to drink water from the well in the courtyard, lest they should be defiled. Generally in a few days this bigotry is broken down, and the Bible-lesson is listened to and the daily text learnt willingly. This is not compulsory, only those who do not do so are told they are losing what gives us peace and joy. Many come and go without any change of heart,

PERSIAN WOMAN IN OUT-DOOR DRESS.
(*A Basket-seller.*)

or even desire for it; others appear deeply interested. Perhaps the notes of a few cases would tell their own tale best.

Khârnum Jân came from a village three days' march from Julfâ. She was paralyzed; gradually she recovered the use of her limbs, but not of her right hand. She was an eager learner, often begging for an extra lesson at night. On April 5th, 1895, she declared herself a Christian and asked for baptism, but was very much afraid of persecution. Her husband came and claimed her, and she was never able to return. Whenever any one came from her village she would send me a note, constantly declaring her faith in "your Saviour and my Saviour." In 1896 she sent for a Gospel for her boy who was learning to read. Her last note, written shortly before her death in February, 1897, was to ask for another book for her boy.

In June, 1893, a village woman came in with a bad abscess; she had brought only a child of eight to help to look after herself and the baby. The following morning she asked me to beat her child, as she would not get up at night to get water for her. Telling the woman I never beat children, I took the little thing out into the courtyard and asked her why she was so unkind to her sick mother. She said she was afraid to get up in the dark for fear the devil should catch her. On asking her if she had never heard of Jesus, the children's Friend, who is always awake and would take care of her, she said she had not. She listened gladly enough, and learnt a simple prayer. The next morning the mother remarked, "You must have beaten my girl hard yesterday, for last night she did not wait for me to ask her for water, but got up and brought it." Calling the child out again, I inquired if it had not been dark during the night. "Oh, yes," she answered, "and when I woke I was frightened; then I remembered Jesus was awake, and said my prayers; then I got up and was not afraid." She would follow from room to room to hear more of " Jesus, *my* Friend." The morning her mother was dismissed she came saying she knew Jesus was in the hospital, but would He be in her village too?

Let me give two more extracts from my diary :—

" September 11th, 1893.—Read Luke xix. 1—10 in the ward to-day. An Isfahan woman said, ' What ! Zacchæus ran ! The rich like things easy and comfortable; the *poor* must run.'

" February 2nd, 1894.—An old village woman, who when in a fit had fallen over a pan of charcoal and was awfully burnt, was carried in. She lingered a few days, suffering much, but was so grateful and nice. ' Tell me of the God of love; I know nothing of Him,' was her frequent remark. The morning before her death she said, ' All my people are dead; I am alone in the world; you also are alone here. We will love one another, my daughter—child of my soul, kiss me, good night.' The old neighbour who had come with her said constantly, ' She will never recover; give her medicine to make her die quickly.' "

Abbas, a little boy with hip disease, came in 1895, a very bright, engaging little fellow. He used to put his little hands in mine " to keep them good " during prayers. At the end he would say, " Now a prayer for me," repeating the words after me, unless the pain was very bad, when he only said, " Yes, God," at the end of each petition. He recovered well. When passing two years later through the village where he lived, he and his mother gave my fellow-worker and me a warm welcome, inviting their friends to meet us at their house for a Bible-lesson.

Dr. Donald Carr arrived at Julfâ on June 20th, 1894. It

PATIENTS ARRIVING AT JULFA HOSPITAL.

is needless to say how glad we were to welcome him.*
He has been the means of wonderfully advancing the work,
his successful operations being a very great attraction, combined with his unwearying kindness to his patients.

Dr. Carr wrote of one, November 30th, 1896: "One
woman I must especially mention, because we are hoping
through her to make an advance in our hospital arrangements by, if possible, keeping her on and training her as a
nurse. Her name is Khurshid. For long she has suffered
from terrible sores all over her body, and was divorced by
her husband for this reason many years ago. She was with
us just a year, and has now come back again with one or
two small wounds still. . . . I only wish we had taken a
photograph of her as she came in, so that we could the
better appreciate the difference. She is now so completely
changed, and from being a poor, wretched creature, a
misery to herself and every one else, she now goes about
looking well and with such a bright, smiling face, always
anxious to help every one else. It makes one's heart glow
to see such a complete regeneration of body, and as we
truly believe, of soul too; and one can only feel that were
there no other results the year's work would not have been
wasted. Our idea is now to keep her staying on indefinitely,
though she is nearly well, and train her as a nurse." This
hope was not to be realized. Khurshid was with us a few
months longer, during which time she led a consistent
Christian life, begging to be allowed to help others: "Let
me wait on them for Jesus' sake"; trying to persuade them
to accompany her to church or Bible-class. The news

* And not less so to welcome Dr. Emmeline Stuart in May, 1897, just
before my return to England. We thank God He has put it into their
hearts to devote their talents and life to the sick and suffering ones in
Persia.

of this was carried to her village, and her father came and took her away, saying his fellow-villagers had threatened to turn him out of his village if he allowed his daughter to remain longer with the Christians. Some weeks later Khurshid sent a message by a neighbour (who was coming for medicine for herself) that she was endeavouring to serve Christ amid great difficulties. Since then we have had no news of her.

Will you pay a visit to the Bible-classes for Moslem women and children held on Sunday afternoons for all who like to come, and on Mondays and Thursdays for inquirers only? What solemn hours those have been, trying to lead the lost ones to their Good Shepherd, or build up the faith of those who were just beginning to follow Him, and finding the road very rough. The first to join was the grandmother of a little sick boy in our street. Soon she brought her two daughters; they have none of them confessed Christ openly; grannie often says she is trusting to Jesus, but "I am old, how can I confess Christ, when probably they will stone me to-morrow?" Tootie, an old woman almost blind, was the next. She had come to beg one Sunday morning just as I was going to church; I invited her to go with me, which she did. During the sermon, the subject of which was Christ the one Mediator between God and man, she kept saying, "God forbid! I never heard such a thing before." She became a regular attendant both at church and class. One day she said, "I used to be always worrying; now I try to trust God and tell Him my troubles." During her last illness I visited her frequently; the last day she said, "I am so tired, and have no one to nurse me." As I raised her she put her arms round my neck, and lay like a tired child in my arms. I told her she was dying, and asked if she were afraid. "No, I am trusting Jesus, not

Mohammed." She repeated her favourite text, 1 Tim. i. 15, and a short prayer, and then fell asleep. When I went again, the neighbours said she had passed away in her sleep.

Another member of the class asked, "How big a sin can Christ cleanse? I did something awful years ago" (poisoned the child of her fellow-wife). "I don't think He could cleanse *that*; He might the rest."

One Sunday, when in the course of lessons we came to St. Matt. v. 12 to the end of the chapter, the women were deeply interested; some of their comments were, "That was written for us; not to swear falsely. Why, we swear when we know it is not true to gain one *pûl*" ($=\frac{1}{8}$ of a penny). "Divorce only to be on account of sin, not because the woman is ugly or has no family." Another added, "When we hear the Gospel we think we could brave anything, even *die* for Christ; but when men shout at us in the street we are afraid again."

Spies often watched the doors, sometimes beating a member as she left, sometimes not allowing them to enter; but God has never permitted the door to be wholly closed, and has indeed been in our midst, though we were only two or three.

It would not be the whole truth to tell only of the joy and not mention the trouble and bitter disappointment connected with this work; though naturally one feels the "Man of sorrows" is the One to whom one should carry the cases of those who are so far beyond our aid. The missionary's keenest sorrow is when those who seem as if they were starting or had started on the narrow way, turn aside, either becoming careless and hardened or open enemies.

Even from among the members of our Bible-class three have had to be dismissed, it having been clearly proved that their only intention in coming was to spy and report. One of these was at one time one of the most hopeful of the inquirers; so quick and intelligent, fearless in speaking before others, willing to bear a considerable amount of persecution; being at one time cast out of her village, and obliged to take refuge with a friend in another village some miles away; asking for baptism; answering very well when examined by the Bishop and other missionaries; and yet falling in the hour of trial. After she had, evidently to screen herself, given information against another, she still came, but was quite changed—all her happiness was gone. Once when we had just finished reading St. John xi. she quite broke down, saying, "I see no Saviour but Jesus Christ; the prophets, even Mohammed, cannot save us. The question is, can I confess Christ?" Another time she exclaimed, "I have read the Qur'ân many times, but have not found happiness; I want happiness." God grant that though she has denied Him whom she had declared to be her Master, she may, like Peter, repent and receive pardon. Will you seek this on her behalf? Remembering also to pray for us missionaries, that we may be filled with the Holy Spirit, and be so endued with love, wisdom, and power from on high, that we may never by word or deed bring reproach upon Him whose name we bear; but that men, seeing a consistent life, may take knowledge of us that we "have been" and are "with Jesus," and may glorify our Father which is in heaven.

A PERSIAN WOMAN.

CHAPTER VI.

ISFAHAN.

"ISFAHAN, the ancient capital of Persia": this is the one idea we gained from our geography in the long ago.
Were you to visit it to-day, you would see at once much of its glory was gone; several of the *mahallahs* (divisions or districts) on the east of the town are completely ruined; and even in the midst of it houses roofless and despoiled are quite common. The market-place is large. The Prince Governor's palace is on one side; the barracks and two large mosques occupy the other three. We are not allowed, being "Christian dogs" (remember, a dog is an unclean animal in Persia), to defile these sacred places by entering, but the exteriors are very fine, especially that of the "King's Mosque," with its minarets, dome, and frontage covered with tiles, the

dominant colour being a rich blue, relieved by patterns in pale blue, gold, white, &c. Oh, when will our King Jesus be worshipped there? Opening out of the market-place are the covered bazaars, extending a mile across the town. They are so picturesque: the vaulted roofs, and the crowded thoroughfares where camels, horses, mules, donkeys, men, women, and children, all struggle to pass each other. The boys and men are fond of bright colours; green, blue, orange, salmon, dark crimson, are all used for coats, and are set off by white turbans. The women wear dark indigo chuddars and long white veils. The former all shout, "Take your foot away," "Watch," "Look out," "Give way." The shops on either

BRASS WORKERS, ISFAHAN.

side are all open, built in tiers, the better to display the goods; the shopkeepers, seated, carry on the endless bargaining. Truthfulness is at a discount; he who swears and lies most successfully makes the largest profit and is the most thought of.

The first bazaar is for shoes of all colours, then groceries, draperies, fruit and vegetables, carpets, saddlery, &c. The prettiest and most interesting are perhaps the brass bazaar, with its deafening clang of hammers; the cotton one, with the big open baskets of cotton pods, and the pure white wool when it has been picked and beaten out (see next page); and the colour bazaar, where saucers full of ochres of every shade are displayed. The "old bazaar," where second-hand goods of every description are sold, is more curious than beautiful. The streets are, as a rule, very narrow, with rough cobble stones, holes, open cesspools, and often a "jūbe"—i.e. stream or ditch for conveying water for irrigating the gardens—running down the middle or side. Each mahallah is walled off and has heavy doors, which are generally shut at night. The houses are all built of mud or sun-dried bricks, with flat roofs, and no windows facing the street—partly, the people say, for safety, and partly to prevent the women being seen unveiled. Fountains are numerous, and are often considered sacred, the people going to them to vow. The custom is for the people to give a small sum to the mullā or sayyid in charge, fasten a thread on to the lattice-work or some other part of the fountain, vowing, if God will hear and grant a favourable answer to their petition, they will give money or food to the poor, go on a pilgrimage, &c., &c. When the answer is granted they go on "Friday's Eve" (Friday is their holy day), buy a candle from the mullā, light it, and leave it to burn as an offering, and detach the thread fastened at the time the vow was made.

BEATING OUT COTTON WOOL.

But our object in visiting Isfahan is not merely travellers' curiosity, but a desire to see what the Lord is doing and how His cause is being promoted there.

Mrs. Bishop wrote* in 1890 of the way she had been hooted at as she rode through the town by an angry crowd, describing it as "a bad half-hour." When she went to visit one of the wealthy families, an escort of servants was sent for her, that she might not be insulted. Now (1898), thank

* *Journeys in Persia and Kurdistan.*

Opposition Giving Way.

God, the *lady* missionaries as well as the gentlemen visit there a great deal, and opposition seems steadily being broken down. "This is the Lord's doing, and it is marvellous in our eyes." There have been troublous times, and doubtless will be again; it is not likely the devil will surrender such a stronghold without a struggle; but may we not even now say, "Thanks be to God which giveth us the victory through our Lord Jesus Christ"? Ever bearing in mind the Apostle's next words, "Therefore .... be ye steadfast, unmovable, always abounding in the work of the Lord; forasmuch as ye know that your labour is not in vain in the Lord." Then whenever the cry "Christian dog" is raised it will remind us of our duty to keep close to our Master, humbly following Him; and it will make us feel honoured if we are recognized as His disciples and may share His title, "Nazarene, Nazarene."

My first visit was paid (by advice) in native outdoor costume; but hearing that the people had said I was ashamed or afraid of being known as a Christian, and was trying to gain entrance into Moslem houses in disguise, I thankfully exchanged the Eastern chuddar and veil for an English cloak and veil through which I could breathe, for theirs is suffocating, close "mul-mul" muslin, with only the beautiful embroidery across the eyes, and it must not be raised in the street if any man be in sight. These first acquaintances were bigoted people, who had no wish to hear the Gospel, but a great deal of curiosity to see English dress and hear of our mode of life. We have exchanged visits since. One has read St. John's Gospel, and said, "It is all good teaching, only Jesus was not crucified;" but, alas! so far none of them have realized their need of Him.

The next was a wealthy lady who was very ill. Having tried many native remedies, made several vows, bought and worn extra charms and talismans, without finding any relief, she tried the omen, and as it was favourable, sent for me. God heard our prayers and blessed the simple remedies, and she soon recovered.

Through her, entrance was gained into a good many better-class houses, and she has always remained most friendly, allowing reading and prayer, unless she had visitors whom she could not trust that they would not spread a report that she was listening to Christian teaching; but the love of riches, not always too scrupulously gained, keeps her back. One day she said, "I want happiness, pray that I may have it; but I love, I love money." She was ill again in February, 1896. I requested that Dr. Carr (our medical missionary) might be sent for. She was quite willing herself, but her husband was away, and there was no one to give permission; afterwards it was arranged to send a servant to ask his brother to do so. He first sent the messenger back to know if the lady was really ill, and then wrote, "If there is nothing much the matter send for the doctor you name; if you think her seriously ill, I will *not* give leave, because if I do, and she dies, my brother will say I sent for that doctor to have her killed." The idea of running the risk of blame to save a *woman's* life did not occur to him—women are so little thought of! God, the All-merciful, again heard and answered prayer, and raised her up. Visiting this same lady the following year, just after the death of her husband, I found twenty-five relations in the zenana, all frantic with grief, the widow being held by her slaves to prevent her beating her head against the wall; they listened to St. John xi. Jesus weeping for His friend, sharing the sisters' sorrow, and then giving life and joy, interested them; but Isaiah liii. 4, 5 amazed them. "Would that He bore my sorrow," "And mine," "And mine," they exclaimed.

Eastern Architecture. 59

INTERIOR OF WELL-TO-DO PERSIAN HOUSE.

Would that you could realize the aimless, hopeless, sad lives those Moslem women lead; it would make you long for them to hear of our Saviour's love for them; they are so struck to hear of His caring for women. For example, they said on hearing St. Mark v., "Jesus kept a *rich man* waiting while He healed a *poor woman* who could not pay Him!" Again, when listening to St. John iv., that our Lord, wearied with His journey in the noonday heat (the sixth hour in Persia, as in Palestine, is noon), should have yearned to save a soul would not have surprised them had it been a *man*, but for Him to take the trouble for a *woman* meant to them far deeper love and compassion. Oh, that we, His disciples, may by His enabling power follow His example, and not rest until all *women* as well as men have heard His Message, "Come unto Me, all ye that labour and are heavy laden, and I will give you rest."

The gratitude and affection of many is very touching; to give one or two examples met with when visiting in Isfahan. A young bride (about ten years old) who was very ill whispered, "Let me kiss you. Do be a Moslem." Her mother-in-law said, "Be still; you will vex her." The bride: "Are you vexed? Do believe and be admitted to heaven." After kissing and petting her, I told her how glad I was to think she was my friend, and suggested that we should pray together to the one living and true God for pardon and salvation. Several women were present, and were attentive during prayer and a simple Gospel talk. Many half-hours have been spent in that house teaching, the bride calling her neighbours to come over the flat roofs into her courtyard to listen, often adding, "Only those who will not talk must come, because the Book will be read."

Another, also a bride, but older, when she recovered, invited me to breakfast, which of course was served on a cloth spread on the floor, bread serving instead of plates, and fingers instead of knives, forks, and spoons. It was springtime, and she had arranged the pink Persian roses in patterns all over the carpet. The neighbours who came in were surprised and some much shocked at such an attention being paid to a Christian! Many a noonday hour has been spent in her room, reading to her while the rest of the family were taking their nap. She now has a Gospel, which she says she loves.

In a mullā's house the daughter had met with an accident while on pilgrimage, and was brought back with bad wounds, made worse by neglect. The old mother was in great trouble about her, and grew very friendly when she saw the wounds were healing. One day she said, "My heart boils for you that you are in darkness and do not know the true prophet. Have you never read in the Books of Moses that our prophet Mohammed, peace be upon him, was to come at the end of time?"* "No, I have not." "Have you not read the Books of Moses?" "Every word many times, but never that." "Oh, how can that be?" she exclaimed. "My son, the mullā, says it is written there." "If you will show me where it is written that Mohammed was to come, I will read it carefully," I replied. She ran to the *khalvat* (men's quarters of the house) saying, "I will ask my son at once. I like you; it is a pity you are in darkness." She returned slowly. "My son says he has not time to look just now for the verse, it is prayer-time at the mosque; but he will look, and I will tell you next time you call." "Meanwhile," I replied, "let us pray that God may grant us His Holy Spirit that He may cast out all falsehood from our hearts and lead us into all truth." "That is a good prayer; I will

---

* Referring to Deut. xviii. 15, which Moslems apply to Mohammed.

pray it," she answered. The son evidently warned her not to refer again to the subject. She always listened respectfully, sometimes eagerly, to the narrative of our Lord, the great Physician, going about doing good, but made no profession of Christianity, and about six months later she died.

There are plenty of bigoted people as well as these dear friendly ones. Often I have seen an old rug or cover spread over the carpet where I was to sit, lest, being a Christian, I should defile it. In one such house a wife, in her anxiety to see the works of my watch, came so near that her skirt touched mine. She drew it back, saying to her friends, "Alas! it has touched hers, the dog; I must wash it in running water before prayer-time." They would not allow a gospel to be read in their house, but listened to the repetition and explanation of some verses from Romans v. An old negress slave of this house followed me down the long passage to the door, saying, "Speak to me: you say there is a free gift for all, whether black or white?" She came early to the women's dispensary at Julfa next morning, bringing a message from her mistress that she wished for medicine for the two maids who had fever, but *not* for herself; she would wait to see if they recovered! The negress' face was a study during prayers as she listened eagerly to the message of the Father's love for her. Will she accept it? We can only pray for her.

At one house a repast of fried eggs well sifted over with sugar (served in the frying-pan) and bread was brought for me: as soon as I had taken what I wanted the remainder was carried out. My servant told me afterwards that a little child had run after the maid crying for some of the eggs, but had been told she must not eat it, the dog had touched it, it must be thrown out to the dogs.

Sad Visits.

During Ramadhan, 1895, I was asked to see a mullā's wife who was suffering from bad ophthalmia. On my first visit permission for prayer only was granted. The next time she said, "We tried the omen and it came out good for us to send for you; we tried the medicine and it was good; to-day we should like to hear your Book—perhaps that is good too." When I had read and explained one of our Lord's parables, she said, "We will tell the mullā we have heard the Book, and there was nothing bad in it." Going again some days later, the mullā was standing at the door; he expressed pleasure and gratitude that his wife was better. When I had been sitting in the zenana a few minutes, a little boy brought a message to the women that should I look at their tongues, they must not swallow their saliva, or they would be defiled and their fast spoilt.

But sadder visits than these must be paid; in the hour of anxiety, sorrow, or death, the Moslem faith gives its followers no sure and certain hope nor divine consolation.

To mention one or two cases only.

In one house a woman was weeping bitterly. Two little ones had died of diphtheria within three days, and the only surviving child had sickened with it. When she had heard of the home for little children, and our hope of reunion through the saving merits of Christ, she called her husband, saying, "Sayyid, sayyid, come here; things to make one's heart glad; our children are not lost, we may see them again! Why did no one tell me this before?" The husband asked for a Gospel, but we have no further news of him.

In a very, very poor house where each room was inhabited by a family a woman lay ill, and suffering also from ophthalmia, tortured with the thought that her aged mother and fatherless children were starving. It was touching to hear her promising again and again that if only her eyes could be cured so that she might sew, she would work and pay for medicine; the idea of free treatment was more than she could grasp, or at first believe. She was quite willing for prayer and teaching. When the parable of the lost sheep had been read, the old mother, who had been sitting near the door, rose; coming close, she exclaimed, while weeping bitterly, "I am lost, out in the cold and dark; pray for me." Thank God, He has raised up the widow, restoring the sight of one eye, so that she is able to work for herself and family. Will you unite with us in prayer that the Good Shepherd may seek and find each one of those lost sheep out in the coldness and darkness of Mohammedanism?

Seated on a rich velvet cushion, fanned by her slaves in a beautiful room, was a wealthy lady. The walls of the room were all covered with tiny arches and honeycomb pattern, shaped while the mud plaster of the wall was still soft, and painted in rich colours, crimson, blue, green, gold, purple, all blended in true Eastern style, studded with small stars,

SMOKING THE KALIÄN.

or octagonal-shaped pieces of mirror, the stained glass window draped with white linen curtains. But riches had not brought her happiness. The kaliān (water-pipe) was brought in, and offered first to the guests, then to the members of the family. As the mistress smoked, she explained the comfort she derived from it, and asked how English women could get on without it. I told of Him upon whom we may roll our burdens. For some time she argued that no one's sympathy could have as soothing an effect as tobacco, but gradually she became willing to listen to the glad tidings of a living, ever-present Saviour, able and willing to deliver her from the root of all her sorrows —sin.

We have lingered long in Isfahan, but before leaving, will you wait one minute longer to hear how the devil is endeavouring through his agents to keep the people from a knowledge of the truth? You know very few of the women can read at all, and those who are taught to do so rarely seem to understand the meaning of what they read; this especially applies to the Qur'ân, which they study in Arabic. A Persian doctor's wife in Teheran said she knew of only one woman who could translate either the Qur'ân or her prayers, but added, "Of course, the mullās can, it is their business." On this account teaching is the more necessary, and when in 1894 a good many Isfahani women asked that a dispensary might be opened for them in the town, we gladly acceded, trusting that it might be the means of bringing the Gospel to them. It was started in Bidâbâd (Isfahan) on January 4th; so many came that the mullā's attention was attracted, and hearing that prayer and Bible-reading were given the first place, he closed the doors in February, beating the owner of the house for having let it to us.

Dispensary Work at Bîdâbâd.

In April God opened the way for a fresh effort in Dar Dasht (another mahallah of Isfahan), where for more than six months work was carried on, though not without opposition. Most days, spies sat close to the door to frighten away the women and children, telling them all we wanted was to draw them from the *true* faith. After, the sick would come before daybreak, to gain admittance before their enemies arrived. Others came by the stable door, or over the flat roofs of the neighbouring houses, the very difficulty of coming usually making them more willing to hear the Gospel; some who were well came whenever they could for that alone. In November the mullās and their students from the Moslem college locked the doors, beat the owner for having let it to " foreign infidels," and were waiting with an angry mob to prevent my "defiling the door" by opening it. Many threats were uttered, and the sticks were ready for use, but God restrained the people and delivered me.

It has not yet been possible to continue the work, and for some time even visiting in that neighbourhood was difficult. The boys were told to hoot and pelt me, and what was much more serious, the people were afraid of getting into trouble themselves if they admitted me. But this has passed, and opportunities of telling old patients more of the love of God to them have been granted.

Several men asked for Gospels, to see what was in the Book which their mullās hated and dreaded so much. May we not believe that that Word will not return void?

In August, 1896, when riding through the Dar Dasht bazaar, I came suddenly face to face with the principal mullā; we had not met since the dispensary was closed. After a few epithets needless to repeat, he said, "Why have you come again among the Moslems? Do you not remember I told you you must not?" Of course I took no notice.

Some one said, "She is deaf." So the mullā repeated his remark louder. Finding it still had no effect, he told the boys to call "dog," "Nazarene," &c. They did so down that bazaar only, and no stones were thrown. The following morning the people whom I had been visiting came, saying how grieved they were to hear what had happened, and hoped no difference would be made. God is Almighty: if He be for us, who can be against us? Let us beseech Him to have mercy on all these people, especially on the mullās, that soon a Persian St. Paul may arise to witness for Him.

CHAPTER VII.

SCATTERED SEEDS.

THE towns of Julfâ and Isfahan lie in the centre of a very large plain through which the Zindeh-rûd (living river) flows. All along its course there are numerous villages; at this moment the names of twenty-seven occur to me, all within easy walking or riding distance of Julfâ. Their inhabitants vary very much; some are bigoted and argumentative, others friendly and frank, others very ignorant of their own and all religion. For instance, at one village a woman said, "It is a pity you cannot come every Thursday" (when they have a custom of reading special services in preparation for their holy day, Friday), "and read instead of the sheikh. We can understand your Book, but we cannot his." At a neighbouring village about fifty neighbours gathered in the courtyard of the house where a fellow-worker and I had gone to see a sick woman. They were all attentive during a short address on the publican's prayer; directly it was finished a woman asked us to remain until she returned, and ran quickly out of the courtyard. In about half an hour she returned with an ounce measuring-glass in her hand, which she gave to us, saying, "I stole this from

70   Among the Mountains.

A PERSIAN VILLAGE.

your dispensary last year, but never knew that it was a sin; pardon me." Another inhabitant of this village stated, "You were born a Moslem, but your parents, being Christians, did not bring you up to be one!" In another house there were many curious spectators to see a child's knee strapped with ointment and plaster, and eager inquiries as to who had given all the skin!

If the village headman's or mullā's wife be friendly, it makes such a difference, the common people not being afraid then to ask the missionaries in. Sometimes I have known very poor women apologize for their wretched, dark, comfortless room, and obtain permission from a wealthier friend to take us to their garden or vineyard the next time. When the vines are cultivated in bushes they are not very attractive, but when they are trained over a high, irregular trellis-work they are lovely, and object-lessons abound. Persians are quick and naturally sarcastic. I remember one, just after I had used some pink roses as an illustration of God's superabounding love not merely giving us the necessaries of life, but beautiful flowers to make us glad, holding up a weed with a really lovely little white flower, saying, "Do you call *this* a proof of love?" The sad lesson of sins beautiful as weeds, but equally destructive, was often referred to by the listeners.

In some places only very irregular work was possible, after a few visits the attention and anger of the mullā was sure to be roused, and the workers returned without thanks. On one occasion Miss Braine-Hartnell was not even allowed to ride through a temporarily hostile village to get to another, though since then she has again been allowed to visit (which of course means *teach*) in both. Faith and patience are indeed needed for such sowing.

In Hoseinabad quite a party of women and children had

INTERIOR OF VILLAGE HOUSE—WOMEN SPINNING AND KNITTING.

followed me from the street into a large courtyard, and were sitting quietly listening to the Gospel, when a very old woman came in, asking if the foreigner were there. Being answered in the affirmative, she said, "I have come to see the lost one." Coming close and peering into my face, she added, "Till you believe on Ali[*] you will never go to heaven." I replied, "I thought heaven was *God's* abode." "Perhaps, but until you accept Ali you can never enter there."

She dispersed the group of women, telling them not to listen. More than a year later, on a bitterly cold snowy day I was asked to go into a ruined house to see a dying woman, and at once recognized the disturber of the previous occasion. Poor thing! she had been cast out by her

[*] Mohammed's son-in-law, one of the greatest Emâms.

family as useless, and was in an almost nude condition, lying half covered by dried leaves which had been stored there for fuel. She snatched at a piece of bread a child was eating, and was evidently starving. It was dreadful to hear her crying over and over again, "I am horribly afraid of death; give me medicine to keep me alive." Help had come too late; she lingered a few days, during which time she seemed incapable of understanding the simplest text.

Very different from this was the case of another villager who had asked for reading. When I inquired if there were any particular passage she wished for, her husband, sitting outside in the courtyard, out of sight though not of hearing,

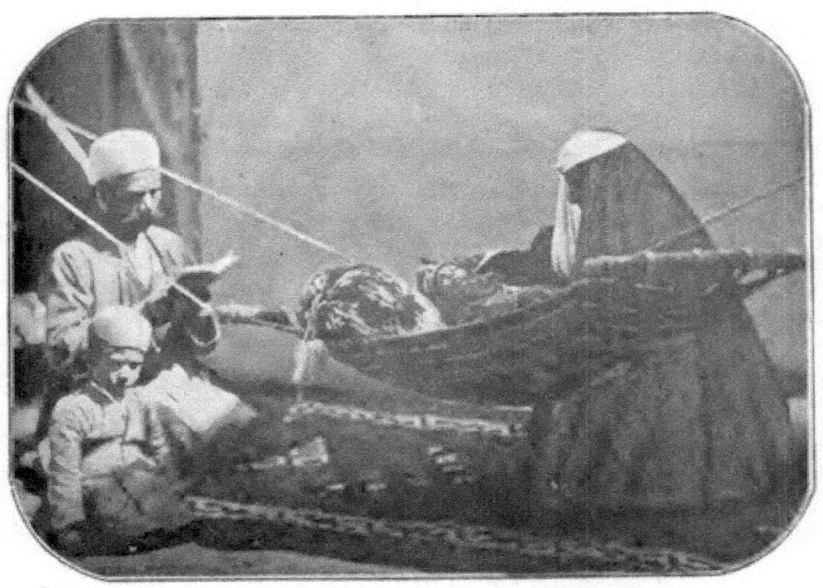

A PERSIAN FAMILY.

replied, "Begin at the beginning; *I* want to hear it all." For months they had a weekly lesson, then the neighbours stirred up much opposition. Though the man still says he is a Christian at heart, he has not come forward to openly confess Christ; the woman was always friendly, but never made any profession of faith in Christ.

At a village not far off a wall fell on a boy; his friends, in their anxiety to dig him out before he was suffocated, cut him dreadfully with their spades. They went for one of their surgeons, who, when he found the case would need much attention and the parents were too poor to pay, declined it. Then in despair they came to the Christians for help. Some of the people who were friendly advised me in a whisper to do nothing, as if the boy died the father would be sure to lay the blame on me. But it was impossible to refuse the mother, weeping so bitterly for her only son fast bleeding to death. Going to the door of the room so that the neighbours who thronged the courtyard should hear as well as those in the room, I told them I would do what I could for the boy, but before beginning we must unite in seeking God's blessing on the means to be used, and beseech Him to grant healing. The people were not silent. There was no time to be lost; seeing a mullā standing in the shadow of the door, I said to him that one word from *him* would quiet the crowd. "Be silent," uttered in the chanting tone used for prayer, was his only reply. The effect was instantaneous, and God, always more ready to hear than we are to pray, heard, and granted our petition.

For over three months that sick room became a meeting-place for many who would have been afraid to come to the Mission for teaching, though since then one has joined the Bible-class. The mullā's boy often ran in to see how the wounds were healing, and one day invited me to go and see his mother, who was graciously patronizing. The boy asked me to give him a Gospel. I told him I would gladly if his mother gave her consent. "I am a *boy*, not a girl," was his indignant reply. "True," I answered, "but God did not say *girls*, but '*children*, obey your parents.'" I do not know which was most surprised, the boy or his mother; but he was permitted to have it. He is very bright and intelligent; oh, that he may become a preacher for Christ instead of (as his family intend) Mohammed. Last year he entered the Moslem theological college to be trained for a mullā.

The father is one of those strange characters, friend and foe by turn. Sometimes forbidding us to enter his village; again, sending if any of his family were ill, and expressing surprise that it was so long since last we called. Such conduct is not uncommon. I was asked to go after sunset to see the baby of one of the greatest spies; he himself watched at the door to see that none of his fellow-spies were in sight. My servant, while waiting for me, asked the man if he were not afraid to let me give medicine to his baby, I might poison her. He replied that he had no fear, as he knew Christians would not do so.

Riding to and from the villages one sees so many of the Bible customs: the oxen ploughing, with only the yoke as harness, to which their burden, the plough, is attached — reminding one of St. Matthew xi. 29, where our Lord uses the simile to teach us that without Him we are as helpless as one ox would be to draw the plough; but, when united, bound to Him, our Almighty Fellow-Worker, nothing is impossible. Two women grinding their corn, sitting one on either side of the millstones; there is a hole in the upper stone, through which they pour the grain, then, both taking hold of the handle, they swing the stone round; the flour falls over the edge of the lower stone into a sheet spread beneath it on the ground. The "watered garden," fresh and luxuriant; whereas the "garden that hath no water" is parched and withered. The cornfields, the reapers, not stacking the corn, but making a great heap of it, which is gradually spread on the ground, when a many-bladed instrument, drawn by a donkey, chops it up; the man, "whose fan is in his hand," standing ready to throw up the chopped wheat, so that the chaff may be blown away, while the grain falls at his feet. The shepherd with the lamb carried on his shoulders. The lengthy salutations. No wonder our Lord,

IN THE HARVEST FIELD.

Visiting a Headman's Wife.

UNEQUALLY YOKED.

realizing more than any that "the King's business required haste," gave the command to His servants about to start on their mission, "salute no man by the way."

Are you too tired to visit one more village before closing this chapter? The headman brought word that his favourite wife was very ill, and asked me to visit her at once, offering to be our guide, as neither I nor my servant had been that way before. The zenana was crowded when I arrived, all the village women having assembled; the poor woman, in accordance with one of their customs, repeating, as each wished her good-bye, "Forgive me." *

The women's curiosity was very great, as they had not seen an English woman before, and their questions were innumerable. "Why have you no ear-rings? Why are you not married? Where is your mother? Tell me how old you are," &c., &c. Reminding them of their sick friend,

* Literally, "make me lawful," "مرا حلال کی."

instead of quieting them as I had hoped, only gave a fresh topic for questioning. "Will you see her? Will you give her the *last* medicine *first*, that she may soon be well? In how many days will you promise to cure her? What! you cannot cure, you have never cured any one? But so-and-so had medicine from you, and recovered, that is why we sent for you." All were listening for the reply, and heard for the first time of the Great Physician with whom are the issues of life and death.

The poor patient was in a very bad state. All I could do was to dress her terrible wounds, and try to make her more comfortable. Then, sitting beside her, I asked if I might read to her. She turned her head away. "No, I am too miserable to listen." But when she heard that the Bible

BREAD-MAKING AND BAKING, PERSIA.

was our source of comfort and joy, she said, "If you know anything that would give me happiness, read that." Afterwards she whispered, "Lady, is it true? Is it for *me* or for you foreigners?" "God's Word," I replied, "says '*Whosoever* believeth,' 'The blood of Jesus Christ His Son cleanseth us from all sin.' Shall we ask Him to give you life everlasting in the land where there is no more pain?" The women were silent enough, only ejaculating at the close of each sentence, "God," "God." Just as I was leaving she whispered, would I come again if she sent for me? I promised, but did not expect to see her again. Two days later, when out visiting, a message was sent, asking me to go the following morning. Before I had gone far up the village street I heard the sound of the people wailing for the dead. The headman met me at the door, and told how his wife had made him promise to send again that I might read to her daughter, as what she had heard had given her some hope and comfort. Passing into the zenana, the first words I heard were part of the weeping service being repeated by a paid mourner, "Weep for the sister who is lost—lost—lost." And the cry was echoed by all present, "Lost—lost." "Weep for the sister wandering in space, weep—weep," and again the friends took up the cry. When this portion of the service was over, the daughter came forward, repeating what her father had previously said. She asked eagerly if I had brought the Book. There was silence for over an hour, while I read and told of Him who is "the Resurrection and the Life."

The headman accepted a Gospel to study with locked doors at night for fear of the mullā.

Will you unite with the sowers in asking that these scattered seeds may one day yield a rich harvest "unto the glory and praise of God"?

CHAPTER VIII.

"STONE MADE READY."

IN 1 Kings vi. 7 we read of "stone made ready," for the building of God's temple. How much lies behind those three words! We know the temple was built and beautifully decorated within and without in seven years from the laying of its foundation; but how much preparation had gone before, so that when the appointed time had come the house of God might be put together without even the jarring sound of a hammer.

We, too, are looking forward "unto an holy temple" to be "fitly framed together," and though we cannot yet see the wall of the Persian court of it rising from the ground, yet, thank God, we do see living stones being "made ready." Of those who may be said to be still "in the rough," the listeners and inquirers we have already thought; but there are four women * who have been built upon the foundation, Jesus Christ, the Rock of Ages.

The first of these was Sakineh, who came in 1893 to the women's dispensary with her aunt, who was ill. At that time Sakineh was a bigoted Moslem, and constantly

* There are, besides these women, baptized male converts; but as this little book deals only with work among women and children, the men are not specially mentioned, though none the less heartily do I thank God for each one of them who, through His mercy, has become a living stone in Christ.

tried to get the medicine for her aunt before prayers, so as not to hear the Gospel. But gradually its message touched her heart, and in spite of herself she listened. When her aunt recovered, she made excuses to return to hear more. In 1894 she came for treatment for herself, her husband's cruelty having made her ill, for which reason he divorced her. Sakineh was then eager to learn more of Christ's love.

On Good Friday, during the Bible-lesson in the dispensary, I remarked, "Would that my Saviour were yours too!" Sakineh replied that she hoped for salvation through Jesus. Every one turned and looked at her in pious horror, invoking the aid of Mohammed, Ali, and Abbas against the "infidel." The women were so angry that she had to leave the room and house at once. Some of them reported the matter to her father, who beat her cruelly; but this seemed to increase her desire for teaching. She joined the Bible-class and came to the Persian service on Sunday mornings.

In the autumn, after seeing an Armenian baby baptized at the morning service, Sakineh said, "Take me to the clergyman, and ask him to baptize me and my baby." She declared her faith in Jesus as the only Saviour, and renounced all faith in Islam. Both Bishop Stuart and the Rev. W. St. Clair Tisdall, who examined her, thought she was trusting simply in Jesus. For the next six months she came regularly to be taught. When warned of the persecution likely to follow her baptism, she replied that she was not afraid, she was willing to die; but hoped grace would be given her never to deny her Lord as Peter did.

On Good Friday, 1895, at a special service at 7.30 a.m., she was baptized, keeping her name Sakineh (light), but her baby's name was changed from Hassan to Abraham. Shortly after she began to try and tell her own family and neighbours the glad tidings she had learned. Soon the news spread in her village, Hoseinabâd, that she was a Christian. Then a system of boycotting and persecution began. Her friends no longer saluted her in the streets; she was pelted with mud and stones, hooted, called infidel, Nazarene, Christian dog, &c. On Saturday, June 22nd, when at the public baths, a woman noticed she had no Moslem charms on, and charged her publicly with being a Christian. At first she was afraid to reply, then answered, "Yes." At once she was cast out, and the place declared defiled by her. She was followed down the street by an angry mob and beaten with a chain used for whipping donkeys. The following Sunday afternoon her mother came to warn her, as she was leaving class, that her enemies were watching for her; but she started bravely, saying, "It does not matter if they kill me, but I hope they will not kill Abraham." No violence was offered her that day. Next day she petted and played with her baby during class. Afterwards she said, "I know I ought not to have played with baby during Bible-lesson, but I am so glad he was not killed yesterday." That night she was cruelly beaten with a chain by her uncle; she was much bruised and cut, but not the least daunted.

On June 30th her fellow-villagers declared either Sakineh must be put to death or she and her parents must leave Hoseinabâd.

The question was raised, ought we to try and protect her in Julfâ? She said, "No! as long as my parents will have me I think it is my duty to remain. I think Jesus has given me a work there." We reminded her of Christ's promise, "Lo, I am with you alway." She replied, "Jesus has often been very near before." She was hooted and struck several times before she reached home, but not injured.

As night came on the mob surrounded the house, threatening to take her life. Her brother-in-law got her and the baby over the wall of the village into the desert, and brought her to our house, and begged that they might be protected. Sakineh was unnerved, but even in her distress kept on repeating, "I have not denied Christ; I want to live and die a Christian." She was with us for three days, and attended the inquirers' class on Monday, urging her friends to be baptized. "I am so glad I have been. Do not be afraid of suffering for Christ's sake."

On Tuesday evening I was detained till late at the hospital, but found her sitting up when I returned, waiting for her Bible and reading lesson. "I want to be able to read the Gospel soon," she said. On Wednesday her mother and a friend came to persuade her to renounce Christianity. When she refused, her mother turned against her, and after using bitter language, left her without the usual salutations and blessings, which tried her sorely. In the afternoon the Kad Khuda (headman) of Hoseinabâd came urging her to return with him and all would be right, but she knew he was not to be trusted. It was thought best to remove her late that evening to Miss Conner's rooms at the hospital. She hardly slept all night, wanting to pray and talk. Once she said, "I know they want my life. I will die for Jesus; I cannot be a Moslem—but do try and save baby's life." She was troubled as to whether she had broken the fifth commandment, but Ps. xxvii. 10 comforted her. "That is for me," she said.

All was quiet till midday on Thursday, when Sakineh's sister came, saying the villagers were determined to kill her. She was anxious to smuggle Sakineh away to a Moslem shrine, and then say she had found her there, which would save her life; but Sakineh was determined. "I will not return; I will die a Christian."

Shortly after, we heard the mullās rallying the people with the trumpet-call, and them replying, "For Ali and God's sake."

We learnt that representatives had been to Isfahan for an order to have Sakineh given up to them, and failing to obtain

WALL SURROUNDING A VILLAGE.

it, had been advised by the mullā (Agha Nejify) to rouse the villagers and return *en masse*, when they would be listened to. Sakineh asked, "Are they after me?" "Yes. Are you afraid?" "No," she replied; "if you asked me to go again now to be baptized, I am ready. I love Jesus more to-day than I did then."

Bishop Stuart and Mr. Tisdall did all they possibly could to protect Sakineh by interviewing leading people, but in vain. The mob was at the doors, bent on murder. When the last hour seemed to have come, God answered our prayers in a marvellous manner, putting it into the heart of the Prince Governor to send an order that Sakineh and her boy were to be given up to him, as the mob could not be restrained, but sending a written promise by the vizier of the *anderun* (zenana) that they should be protected.

It was hard to tell Sakineh. At first she refused to go. "Let me be killed here," she said; but that did not seem right. When told that we thought this was God's answer to our prayer, she took Abraham in her arms and came out quite calmly into the courtyard where the Persian officials were waiting for her.

The Bishop took her hand and gave her to the acting British Agent, Mr. Aganor, and he handed her over to the Vizier. We all went with her to the Julfá gate. The street was crowded with her own relatives, mullās, spies, and villagers, all furious. She passed calmly amidst them all. Half-way up the street she whispered, "What was that text you said last night?" (Ps. xxvii. 10). She repeated it after me, saying, "My father and my mother *have* forsaken me, but the Lord *has* taken me up." At the entrance of the desert the Prince's carriage and escort were waiting, and we had to part, thanking God for the power He had given her to face such a trial, and trusting her to His Almighty protection.

Nearly two years passed without Sakineh being allowed to hold communication with the Mission party. We heard she had been taken before the Prince, and asked in whom she believed, when she confessed Christ, speaking of God and heaven, and looking so happy that those present said she must be mad!

Sometimes we would hear of her through a fellow-servant in the anderun. Once a serving-maid who had come to the dispensary brought a message: "I am the same Sakineh as I was when with you." On my asking the maid if Sakineh were still a Christian, she said she did not know; they were forbidden to talk with her about religion; but added, "Sakineh is not a Moslem; she is not one of us, for she does not lie, and we all do." The next news we had was that she had been re-married to her husband by the Prince's order, but was still in the anderun. On May 27th, 1897, hearing I was returning home on furlough, she made an effort to see me, obtaining leave from the chief of the eunuchs to come out for a few hours; another woman being sent with her to see that she returned. They left the anderun at daybreak and came to the Julfâ Hospital.

Sakineh told me she was not allowed to have a Gospel nor to speak of religion. "But that does not matter, for I have it in my heart." She wore no charms nor talismans, but said the Prince had himself fastened a beautiful silver one inscribed with the Moslem creed on Abraham's arm. She had taken it off, saying her boy was not a Moslem, and though the Prince was angry and every one treated her badly for some time, she remained firm. The church bell rang for the morning service. She insisted on coming again to worship with the Christians, though knowing it was a risk to run. She repeated the Lord's Prayer, Creed, and Commandments perfectly, and the greater part of the

General Confession, whispering, "I say them every day, not to forget." She had to leave directly after service. Her last words were, "I trust Jesus will make me free some day, and let me come back to the Mission."

Her desire has been to a great extent granted. Miss Stuart wrote on June 26th, 1897, "You will, I know, be greatly interested to hear that I had a visit from Sakineh; she came to the hospital to my cousin [Dr. Emmeline Stuart] to get medicine for her throat, which was very bad, and then came here. When I brought out the Gospel, she read quite easily ten or twelve verses of John i. I thought it wonderful she had not forgotten, as she has not been allowed a book. I offered her a copy of St. John, thinking she might be able to use it without attracting attention, but she said no, she could not, but she had it in her heart all the time."

On September 2nd, 1897, at a special service at 7 a.m., Bishop Stuart confirmed Sakineh, with Hamedeh Mariam and Khurshid Martâ, and the following Sunday all three partook of the Lord's Supper.

Mrs. White wrote on December 28th, 1897, "Sakineh has just paid me a visit. She seems so happy in Christ, and tells me she has got two persons she knows to wish to become Christians." May God grant her the joy of leading them to the Saviour and seeing them receive pardon and peace!

Hamedeh was a lying, idle, inveterate little beggar when I first knew her. Sakineh made friends with her, told her of Jesus, and brought her to class. For some time it was evident she had no wish to hear the Gospel, but merely came to please Sakineh. But the day after Sakineh was taken from us, Hamedeh came saying she had been in the street the previous day, and had seen Sakineh pass calmly amid the crowd of angry people who were waiting to put her to death; Hamedeh added, "I am miserable; give me the happiness you have given to Sakineh." After this Hamedeh came regularly for teaching, so eager to learn that often at the end of an hour's Bible-lesson she would grumble at having such a short lesson! Soon there was a marked change in her life; she gave up thieving and lying, and tried to learn to knit and sew. Just three months after she had become a Christian she was seized as she was leaving the Bible-class on Sunday afternoon, and taken before a neighbouring mullā and asked if it were true she had learnt the Christians' prayer. On replying she had, she was warned that should she repeat it she would be beaten. Telling me about it afterwards she said, "It was not hard to get up and repeat my Master's prayer before His enemies, but it was hard to turn a deaf ear to my own mother who had followed me and was kneeling behind me entreating me not to say it"; but, thank God, He gave her power to do so. Immediately after this she asked to be baptized.

For some months I could not get her to pray in her own words. Her first prayer aloud was, "Oh, God, be merciful to me, a sinner. Wash me that I may be whiter than snow. Help me that I may be able to work for Jesus Christ. Amen"—a prayer which has been fully answered. Her greatest happiness is when she can persuade any of her former companions to join the Bible-class. On one occasion some outsiders had come in; Hamedeh had fever, and was lying down, but when she heard some of the members of the class say there was need for secrecy, and it did not matter whether people confessed Christ openly or not, it was quite sufficient if God saw they had love for Him in their hearts, she sat up, saying, "There is no need for

Was She Happy?

secrecy. God can take away fear; I am not afraid of any man now." This was no idle boast; over and over again she has proved its truth, bearing persecution bravely and uncomplainingly for her Master's sake.

One day Hamedeh came in after having been beaten in the street by a Moslem, and then thrown violently against the corner of a wall, so that her arm was all bruised and bleeding; while bathing and bandaging it, I asked her when she was happiest, when she was a Moslem and had no persecution, or now that she was a Christian and had so much to suffer? Looking reproachfully at me, she said, "Happy when I was a Mohammedan? I did not know what happiness meant; I did not know the meaning of the word until I knew Jesus Christ."

A BEGGAR IN A STREET IN PERSIA.

Hamedeh began to attend church regularly in the autumn of 1895, but until the spring of 1896 sat during the whole service, so as not to attract attention. Then she felt this was wrong and began to adopt Christian customs and join in the service, learning the Lord's Prayer, Creed, Ten Commandments, General Confession and Thanksgiving, and the Canticles, &c., by heart, as at that time she could not read. One Sunday morning an Armenian baby was baptized. Hamedeh and Khurshid (see Chap. V. p. 49) followed the service carefully; they began to cry, asking, "Why should that baby be baptized, and we are kept waiting?" But in a minute Hamedeh said, "That baby is only receiving the *sign;* we have the *root* of the matter." In July, 1896, Hamedeh was twice beaten by spies in the streets and threatened with death, but her faith was not shaken, as she herself said, "I am not afraid; I am a Christian. If I am killed to-night, know that I am one of you."

The time of persecution, which began in January, 1897, was a very solemn sifting time, any who had come with the hope of earthly gain falling away, while the few faithful ones seemed only the more anxious for instruction, and none more so than Hamedeh. One day she came in looking bright. When some Moslem visitors who were with me had left, she told me that she had heard that her name had been entered for death, and asked me to tell Bishop Stuart, and beg him to baptize her at once. "I want to keep Christ's command before I die and have to meet Him in Heaven. If I am killed, remember I am a Christian though I am not baptized." Then, kneeling down, she prayed for her own family first, and then for her enemies by name, beseeching that they too might learn to believe in Jesus and find salvation.

For some weeks she was unable to come to us, owing to

the great vigilance of the spies; when she returned her joy was great. She said she had been marvellously preserved; several times enemies had come saying they would take her to Isfahan, as they wanted her head, but she had not even been beaten.

The Rev. C. H. Stileman (our Secretary) examined Hamedeh before her baptism, and was very pleased with her grasp of the truth, and on Sunday, May 16th, 1897, she was baptized in the presence of all the Mission party, taking the name Mariam as well as Hamedeh. Many times during the day she said, "This is a glad day for me," and still says so, though she has had much to bear for the Master; petty daily annoyances, often more wearing to the spirit than even the great trials. For example, her neighbours would not let her draw water from the well in the compound, because her hand would defile the rope. If she were recognized in the market-place, no one would buy the socks she had knitted, the women whispering to each other not to buy them because her hand was unclean.

Since my return to England Miss Braine-Hartnell has written several times of Hamedeh Mariam's courage. In a letter dated June 12th, 1897, Miss Braine-Hartnell says, "Hamedeh has been roughly handled again by the cobbler when she was near the hospital; both her arms were swollen and bruised, poor child. But she says if I forbid her to come here on account of persecution she will not tell me if she is hurt again." August 14th: "Hamedeh has had the money I had paid her for her work stolen from her, and again her arms bruised." October 9th: "Last Sunday, just when the converts were at the Communion, some Moslems got into the gallery, and it was soon known they had been seen in the church. In the afternoon Hamedeh was again knocked about and bruised; poor girl, she was in great pain on Monday, but said she would venture to church again next Sunday." November 27th: "Hamedeh goes on well; she has lately been going to visit the little girl who was her neighbour, and who is now married. I think it was very plucky of her, but she has a truly missionary spirit, and is always anxious for others to hear of Christ." February 26th, 1898: "Poor little Hamedeh is often troubled about marriage; her family have been trying hard to get her married to various people, but she will have none of them. Of course, it is very hard for her mother (her father died many years ago), for she remains poor, but it is very hard for the child too."

Dr. Emmeline Stuart wrote on March 19th: "The poor little convert, Hamedeh, is having a bad time of it at present. Her relations are wanting to marry her to a Mohammedan, and she refuses. She got some beatings in consequence last week from her uncle, and on Wednesday a farrâsh (policeman) was sent for her, and she was taken before the deputy-governor of Julfa. He said he had heard she had left her religion. If it was *not* true what people said, he would do nothing to her; if it was *true*, he would. She answered that it was perfectly true that she had left her religion, and that they could do what they liked to her. So he sent for the sticks, and she was beaten there and then. She says that the answer was just given to her at the time, a literal fulfilment of the promise, 'It shall be given you in that hour what ye shall speak.' She is so young, only seventeen, it is dreadful she should have to suffer like this. Oh, for religious liberty in this land!"

Miss Braine-Hartnell wrote again on April 8th: "Hamedeh has been in hospital for the last ten days, waiting on one of her neighbours who has had a cataract removed. I am very thankful she has been sent here. The poor child has been

Constant Trouble. 93

very much persecuted lately. No less than four times she has been beaten by her uncle; he keeps on trying to force her to be married, and she steadily refuses. She yesterday returned a ring that was given her, and I quite expect she will pay for it, but her courage keeps up. She says they may beat her or kill her, but she will not marry a Moham-

COOKING IN THE STREET IN A PERSIAN CITY.

medan, and her mother will not hear of letting her go to Teheran or anywhere else." May 28th: "Hamedeh has been in constant trouble lately; for three weeks her mother was separated from her, and carried off by her brother, and Hamedeh was sheltered at night by her kind neighbour, but she has got her mother back now. This week the Nazib threatened to take them both to town to the mullā, but Mr. Stileman sent him a message to say he had better be careful; and he has dropped the matter. As it is so near the tenth of Moharram (the great weeping-day for Hosein, always a fanatical time), we have told Hamedeh to stay away until that date is passed. I hear she is grieving very much over this. She has plenty of courage to confess Christ."

The following extracts are translated from letters received from Hamedeh, and tell a little of her own feelings. September 4th, 1897: "Please God, your health is good, and the peace of God is with you, by the help of our Lord Jesus Christ, peace is ready. You know that in Persia it is difficult for us; it does not matter, for Jesus Christ's sake; if it be persecution, I am content. Mariam Hamedeh says we pray that God may give us strength. . . . On Thursday the Bishop Sâhib laid his hand (i.e. confirmed) upon the head of Mariam Hamedeh, and Khurshîd Martā, and Sakineh, and we prayed. When your letter came I was very glad, and I remembered that on Sunday when I was in church my hand was in yours and tears fell from my eyes. Now I sit alone in church, but we are not alone; I know our Lord Jesus Christ is near us. If you were not in church your spirit was with me. . . . Next Sunday Sakineh, Khurshîd Martā, and Mariam Hamedeh may go to the Holy Communion." January 8th, 1898: " . . . Oh, dear mother, sometimes I feel sorry that I am not able to see you, but again I am thinking that though I cannot see you now, or perhaps death may take me to gain, I know that I can see you in heaven with my Saviour, and there we will be happy for ever. . . . I think you will be very sorry to hear that a few weeks ago I got a very bad sore throat [diphtheria], but again God spared me. I am sure He has much work for me to do, and to be a true witness for Him. Thank God that now I know and I believe that the Almighty God is my Saviour. Oh, I wish that hundreds of my nation might believe the same Jesus can forgive their sins, and only He can wash their sins with His precious blood and bring them from darkness into His bright light. . . . I think you will remember the friend who lived in our house; she was married three weeks ago. Very often I am going there to talk with her. Once I spoke with her of St. John iii. Please pray for me, that I may be a light in this hard place." March (no date given): "Oh, my dear mother, I know Jesus Christ has given me health. I know our Lord Jesus Christ will be with us. I am very grateful to Dr. Lady (Dr. Emmeline Stuart), and Teacher Lady (Miss Braine Hartnell), who took care of me (literally turned their face toward me). We know that in the midst of troubles Jesus Christ will be with us. In the midst of the troubles which I see, there is one joy for me. For a long time I have prayed for my mother, that her faith may be perfect. Oh, mother, in this country we are great strangers. Oh, mother, for some time I am in the house of my maternal aunt, for my own mother does not very much wish me to be near her, and does not eat food with me, and my mother's brother once beat me. This I know afresh in the midst of these troubles, there is one joy for me, our Lord Jesus Christ will be our gracious and merciful Father. He has Himself said, 'I am with you alway, even unto the end of the world.' Oh, mother, certainly pray for me. I am very

ONE OF HAMEDEH'S LETTERS.

glad that your coming is near. Would that when you come you and I may sit alone in the house and read the Book. Often when I go to church your place, oh, mother, is very empty before me. I think that in this country we are great strangers. 'I'm but a stranger here'" [here she has copied the hymn in Persian]. "I know that in Persia I have three friends: one Goher, one Sultân, one Mah Sultân. Sometimes I go to —— Before my friend I read the Book. I know that, except these three, I have no friends in Persia. Certainly I know that all the ladies (missionaries) are my friends. Oh, mother, we are weak; we must pray that the Lord may give us more (grace) that we may be able to give the news to others. Would that you were near me, that you might know what sorrow I have. Our Lord Jesus Christ has said, 'Where two or three are gathered together in My Name, there am I in the midst of them.' He has said, 'I will not leave you orphans, I will come to you.' I eat a great deal of sorrow, because great lady (Mrs. White) is going away from me to Yezd, but our Lord Jesus Christ is always near us. Oh, dear mother, I am very glad that your coming is near, and I pray a great deal for you, oh, mother. I have by letter made little conversation [corresponded] with you. I hope till you come to make conversation with you. And I send my salaams to thy mother, and sisters, and friends, and say Mariam Hamedeh says to your mother to give you a kiss instead of me. Again, many salaams to thy mother and sisters, and say, pray much for me, and you also do so. The Lord is my Helper, I shall not be afraid. My maternal aunt and thy friends send many salaams. Oh, mother, I have no sorrow. I wish that we may sit together and read the Book. Would that when you come we may sit together in church. It is a long time that your place is empty, especially on Sunday and Monday [when she used to attend the Bible and inquirers' classes]. Would that God may cause all the inhabitants of Persia to believe. I will never forget you, oh, mother. I also send salaams to you.— MARIAM HAMEDEH."

She wrote again in May: ". . . If you inquire of my state, it is peace. In this country I have trouble. My uncle has beaten me several times, but I have this one joy, Christ and the Holy Spirit will be always near me. Oh, mother, pray much for me, because of our own strength we cannot do God's work. Pray for my mother that she may desire salvation. I also pray that she may not make me marry. The Lord is my Helper, I will not fear. I am not ashamed of the Gospel of Christ, for it is our strength. I thank God that the Lord has given me this courage, that I can say to the accuser, or to every one I can say, 'There is none other Name under heaven given among men whereby we must be saved.' This has not been of my own strength, but it has been of our Lord Jesus Christ's strength. Would that all the inhabitants of Persia believed, ' How sweet the Name of Jesus sounds' [here she quotes the first two verses]. For the few Persian women who are friends, I read the Book. God grant them courage not to fear their husbands, but to come to the lady's house [for teaching]. . . . We are weak; I have no power. I pray much for you; also pray much for me, that I may be able to give the news of the Gospel. Pray also for my mother that she may believe. Mariam Hamedeh, your child, sends her salaams. Whatever trouble I have it does not matter."

How the brave girl's simple, trustful words make one long to be able to shield and protect her! But, thank God, she is safe in our Father's keeping, for Christ has declared, " They shall never perish. . . . No man is able to pluck them out of My Father's Hand."

Khurshíd had been suffering from her eyes for a long time before she came to the women's dispensary in 1896; the sight was almost destroyed, and the pain often very severe. She came week after week, and from the first listened eagerly to the Gospel. After some months she was admitted to the hospital, her patience and cheerfulness were wonderful, and her resignation when she heard there was no hope of recovery; but, thank God, as she afterwards dictated in a letter to me, " I have found a better and brighter light than the one I came in search of."

The daily text was her delight, not merely to be the first

to repeat it correctly, but to understand its meaning; she enjoyed the Bible-readings in the ward and the Sunday Bible-class. One Sunday she asked that the account of our Saviour's crucifixion, which she had not heard, should be read. She sobbed when she heard of His dying love, and remained after class and definitely gave herself up to Him. Mariam Hamedeh, who was then preparing for her baptism, would sit beside Khurshíd repeating what she had learnt from the Gospel. After some time Khurshíd asked for baptism, saying that she was now rejoicing in her blindness, as it had been the means of bringing her to the Light. She received regular religious instruction, and learnt to read the Gospel of St. John as fast as Miss Braine-Hartnell could prepare it for her according to the Braille system. After some months she again requested to be baptized; the Bishop examined her, and was well satisfied that she had accepted Christ as her Saviour.

During the preparation time before her baptism Khurshíd's faith was tested by persecution; spies reported that she came to church, and also to learn to read. She was taken before one of the civil rulers in Isfahan, where she was detained for a fortnight on bread and water in a kind of imprisonment. Afterwards, in consideration of her blindness, she was sent home to her brother, who told her not to come to church for a week or two, but she came straight back to her classes, and is now again going to church.

On September 2nd, 1897, she was baptized Khurshíd Martā, by Bishop Stuart, before the Mission party and other converts, and was afterwards confirmed with Sakineh and Mariam Hamedeh, and partook of the Lord's Supper on September 5th.

One of those present wrote: " Khurshid gave her answers

so clearly and brightly. She certainly has a very clear grasp of the truth, and seems quite to understand that the Holy Spirit must teach her spiritual things."

The translations that I now am about to give are from letters dictated by Khurshíd and written for her by a boy living in the same courtyard, who is himself studying the Gospel:—

". . . Last Thursday, when your letter arrived, I received the name of Khurshíd Martā in the church. The Bishop Sáhib made the sign of the Cross on me, and I received baptism. I am very glad. You know that I am not ashamed of the Gospel, because God's salvation is on those who believe on it. If God be for us, who can be against us? . . . Sakineh sends her salaams, and says I am nearly free; I have come several times to church."

On the outside of the envelope of the next is written, "Martā says, God is love, and I am abiding in His love." The letter is as follows: "Oh, my dear sister, please God your state is good. When your letter reached me I became very glad. I am very grateful that you pray for me because I am near the temptations of the devil. Thanks and praise be to God who gave me salvation from the devil's temptations, and the Lord will take my hand, and will not allow him to defile me in sin. He is my Refuge, and Shelter; then I will not fear. It is evident to me that our strength is in the righteousness of our Lord Jesus Christ, for God and His Son our Lord Jesus Christ with the Holy Spirit are the one living God and will reign for ever and ever. Our duty is to follow our Lord Christ, and without Him we can do nothing. Martā sends many salaams, and says pray much for me, and give my salaams to thy mother and thy two sisters. All your friends send salaams. I am very glad when you give the reply to this letter, write for me in how many more months you will come to Persia. Some days after New Year's Day my lady (Mrs. White) will go to Yezd, and I shall be very sorry. Spiritual songs [i.e. hymns], song the third, 'I'm but a stranger here.'" Khurshîd quotes the whole hymn.

In her last letter she says: "May God protect you from evil. Please God your health is good and the peace of God is with you. . . . Whenever you are engaged in prayer pray for me, I am very grateful to you. God fill me with the Holy Spirit, that I may forsake the temptations of the devil. I hope in Jesus Christ that by the power of God I shall conquer. With the devil I am a sheep without strength. The Lord is our Shepherd; we shall lack nothing. Oh, my sister, thank God that the Lord has heard thy voice and has called me." Thank God that He has opened the blinded eyes of faith to see Him in all His glory.

On April 3rd, 1898, *Gauhar*, the fourth Persian female convert, was baptized by Bishop Stuart. Miss Stuart, who from the time of Gauhar's first visit to Julfâ has been her teacher and friend, wrote this interesting account of her:— *
"It is now more than two years since I first knew Gauhar. The name means 'a jewel.' God grant that she may be one when He maketh up His jewels! She had been staying at the hospital with one of her little girls who had got a needle into her knee and was there for treatment. Gauhar used to come constantly to see me, and very soon began to ask for teaching. She was at that time an extremely ignorant woman, but seemed to have grasped the idea of the need of a Saviour, and her thirst for teaching was almost insatiable. She continued to come to Julfâ at intervals to be taught, and on our frequent visits to her village for a week at a time,

* *C.M. Intelligencer*, June, 1898.

she would spend all her time with me. Her boy she committed to us for schooling, as her great desire was that he should have a Christian education and be able to read the Gospel always to her; so we boarded him with an Armenian, and he attended the Persian school daily, and made good progress for a year, when the school was for a time broken up by Mohammedan fanaticism; but I am thankful to say that the school has been reopened within the last six months, and the boy is living with us under my immediate care, along with another little boy who also attends school.

"Gauhar being largely dependent on her own exertions for support [she weaves canvas and cloth for the women's chuddars], has not been able to spend more than a month at a time in Julfá for instruction; but she has managed to learn a great many verses by heart, and also to read a little from the New Testament, and has improved so wonderfully in intelligence that she herself says that she considers that is God's miracle for her, that He has given her the power to understand. She has even been able so far to instruct her husband that he too is now desiring baptism.

"She has had to suffer a great deal of persecution of late, having been turned out of one house and again nearly turned out of another by the animosity of the neighbours. If her little girl goes to drink water from the well, they say she is defiling it. However, none of these things have shaken her determination to profess Christ and be received into His outward and visible Church.

"We do ask all friends at home to pray very earnestly for this new convert, that she may grow in grace and be kept by God's mighty power from all the temptations and dangers in this land of darkness and cruelty."

It is needless for me to add more. We have seen that "The Lord's hand is *not* shortened that it cannot save;

neither His ear heavy that it cannot hear." He is as able to save Moslems in the nineteenth century as the inhabitants of Judæa, Asia Minor, &c., in the first. But—" How shall they (Moslems) believe in Him of whom they have not heard?" We are "put in trust with the Gospel"; dare we hold it back from those who are perishing for lack of it?

Our Lord's dying prayer for His enemies rings down through the ages as sadly true to-day as when first uttered: "Father, forgive them, for they *know not* what they do." Will you too plead with our Father, "Forgive *them*," and "mercifully forgive the sins of *Thy people*," for they have failed to keep the sacred trust Thou didst commit to them;

A MOHAMMEDAN SCHOOL.

they have not kept Thy command, "Let him that heareth say, Come." Let us humbly entreat God to pour down His Holy Spirit upon each one of us who has dedicated himself, or herself, "manfully to fight under His (Christ's) banner against sin, the world, and the devil; and to continue Christ's faithful soldier and servant unto his, or her, life's end," that being roused to a sense of our high calling, we may no longer delay, but unfurl that banner on which the one word which comprehends the whole of our religion is inscribed, "*Love ;*" for "God is Love," and "This commandment have we from Him, that he who loveth God love his brother also."

THE END.

GILBERT AND RIVINGTON, LIMITED, ST. JOHN'S HOUSE, CLERKENWELL, E.C.

www.ingramcontent.com/pod-product-compliance
Lightning Source LLC
Chambersburg PA
CBHW031405160426
43196CB00007B/903